"Sandra Ingerman's *The Book of Ceremony* and brings it into the modern world to hel ourselves, the divine, and each other. This e map of the territory and a wise guide to sh... clear examples and many wonderful stories and practices. If there was a university for shamanism, this book would definitely be on the core mandatory reading list."

HEATHERASH AMARA
author of *Warrior Goddess Training* and *Awaken Your Inner Fire*

"In *The Book of Ceremony*, Sandra Ingerman explains that ceremony directly connects us to the invisible, sacred realms and helps us achieve joy, peace, and transformation. Ingerman stresses the importance of incorporating ceremonies into our everyday lives as individuals, but also shows that we can use them to bring ourselves together with others in community. More experienced shamanic practitioners as well as beginners at working in the shamanic realms will find a cornucopia of powerful ideas here for creating and engaging in ceremonies that provide a sense of meaning, healing, and connection."

CARL GREER, PHD, PSYD
author of the bestselling, award-winning *Change Your Story, Change Your Life*

"Ceremony means performing a sacred act. During a ceremony, the veil between the worlds dissolves and the gates to our soul open while the hands of our ancestors cradle us. Hope, healing, and miracles all live in this place. As Sandra says in this book: ceremony is a sacred tool so powerful that we cannot keep it for ourselves—it must be shared! Thank you, Sandra Ingerman, for giving the world a book that preserves the mystery of ceremony yet tells us how ceremony is actually done, allowing all of us to taste a drop of eternity."

IMELDA ALMQVIST
international teacher of sacred art and shamanism, author of
Natural Born Shamans: A Spiritual Toolkit for Life and *Sacred
Art, a Hollow Bone for Spirit: Where Art Meets Shamanism*

"There is more to this reality than meets the eye, and the seasoned soul seeker relies on sacred ceremony to dispel illusion and see the whole truth. In *The Book of Ceremony*, Sandra opens the vault and shows us step by step how to design and perform shamanic rituals that peel back the veil and give way to divine guidance. If you are looking for a portal into your highest self—read this book."

NICK POLIZZI
author of *The Sacred Science: An Ancient Healing Path for the Modern World*

"Sandra Ingerman's *The Book of Ceremony* masterfully weaves the earliest wisdom and sacred principles of the natural world into modern life. This book is an extraordinary read for anyone wanting to peer into this ancient form of communication and participation underlying our common reality. She inducts the reader into this sacred field through her stories, descriptions, and instructions, and allows us a glimpse into the underlying mystery that shamans are called to work with. This is not a 'how-to' book, but a chance for readers to see this world through her eyes, learn from her knowledge, and respectfully engage in ceremony on their own."

ANN MARIE CHIASSON, MD
co-director of the Fellowship in Integrative Medicine program at
the University of Arizona Center for Integrative Medicine, and
author of *Energy Healing: The Essentials of Self-Care*

"Laboratory studies show us that focused minds can influence physical reality in surprising ways. Science is just beginning to understand the nature and scope of mind-matter interactions, but for tens of thousands of years, shamans around the world have known how to enter states of awareness that optimize these reality-bending effects. The time-honored way is through ritual or ceremony. Sandra Ingerman's *The Book of Ceremony* captures the wisdom of the ancient shamans. It provides an excellent, modern guide to performing effective ceremonies for many purposes and occasions."

DEAN RADIN, PHD
chief scientist of the Institute of Noetic Sciences and author of *Real Magic*

"*The Book of Ceremony* is a gem! Sandra Ingerman's radiance shines through-out this book. She inspires with an intimate look at her own personal ceremonies. And with clear instruction and support, for those with or without shamanic experience, she gently guides us in creating meaningful and beautiful ceremonies of our own. Guaranteed to become a touchstone of your spiritual library."

MARA BISHOP, MS
author of *Inner Divinity: Crafting Your Life with Sacred Intelligence* and *365 Journeys: Shamanism for Every Day*

"*The Book of Ceremony* is a beautiful, profound exploration of the sacred nature of ceremony. What I love about this book and Sandra Ingerman is that you are invited to go deep—to connect to nature and your deepest essence as a human being and spiritual being through the vehicle of ceremony. This book can be a lifelong and trusted guide to the sacred rituals you create in your life."

JUDITH ORLOFF, MD
author of *The Empath's Survival Guide*

"In *The Book of Ceremony*, Sandra Ingerman has created something I've never encountered before! Sandra offers instruction and examples for ceremonies that apply to virtually any life situation or circumstance I could imagine. And paradoxically, the book feels concise and to the point. Sandra's loving reverence for the earth and all beings is evident on every page, and it's obvious that she is a teacher who 'walks the walk' with immense integrity and authenticity. For anyone interested in shamanism, shamanic practice, and earth-based spirituality, *The Book of Ceremony* is a 'must-have'!"

BYRON METCALF, PHD
transpersonal psychologist and author of *The Shaman's Heart Meditation Training Program*

"Once again, I am moved by the way Sandra Ingerman gifts her readers with her lucid yet profound principles of spiritual living, encouraging us to create beautiful ceremonies that speak to our need to reconnect with the sacred in our modern Western culture. Sandra reminds us as we enter the dreamtime in sacred ceremony, we enter the space where intentions are planted like seeds that will grow into actualities if we nourish them in ceremony. In creating ceremonies that are filled with the presence of love and light, we naturally draw people and even our household pets into enjoying the vibration of the sacred space. I give thanks to Sandra for decades of work and experience, her innovations, her humility, her groundedness, her compassionate teaching spirit, her joyous heart, and the great care she invests in all she writes and all she teaches."

C. MICHAEL SMITH, PHD
psychologist, shamanic teacher, author of *Jung and Shamanism
in Dialogue*, director of Crows Nest Center for Shamanic Studies
International, and teaching member of the *Cercle de Sagesse*

"Shamanism is an ancient spiritual tradition in which shamans use their own body and mind to create a bridge between the personal world of form and the transpersonal world of spirit. They do this with ceremony, and when this bridge is formed, it allows the healing gifts and the power of the spirits to flow across that connection and into our world. Sandra Ingerman is a master shamanic teacher who reveals how performing ceremony may bring the sacred into our ordinary lives. *The Book of Ceremony* is a gift, enabling us to open a line of connection between our self and the power of the universe to manifest healing and our soul's desires in these times of change."

HANK WESSELMAN, PHD
anthropologist and author of *The Re-Enchantment: A Shamanic
Path to a Life of Wonder*, *The Bowl of Light: Ancestral Wisdom
from a Hawaiian Shaman*, and the Spiritwalker Trilogy

"This beautiful book moved me deeply and inspired me to bring more sacred ceremony into my life. Sandra brings such love, compassion, and gentleness to this book that we can't help but be drawn into the profound experience that ceremony brings into our lives. *The Book of Ceremony* not only teaches us so many ways to bring sacred ceremony into our lives, but it also creates a deep desire to tap into our creativity to develop our own unique ceremonies. The way you live your daily life will be forever changed by this book."

MARGARET PAUL, PHD
co-creator of Inner Bonding® and bestselling author of *Do I Have to Give Up Me to Be Loved by You?*, *Inner Bonding*, *Healing Your Aloneness*, and *Diet for Divine Connection*

"*The Book of Ceremony* is a brilliant exposé on how to participate with nature and the unseen spiritual dimensions to generate goodness, harmony, and healing for ourselves and our planet. Guiding us with abundant insights and easily applied practices and tools, Sandra shows how we can each reclaim the natural alchemical powers we are born with to bring about positive change for us and the earth."

LLYN ROBERTS, MA
award-winning author, cofounder of the Olympic Mountain EarthWisdom Circle and Shamanic Reiki Worldwide

"Sandra Ingerman invites you on a life-transforming magical carpet ride in her new release, *The Book of Ceremony*. She reminds you that rituals and ceremonies are the drawbridges to a lush landscape where the ordinary can seamlessly evolve into the sacred. Easy-to-follow directions will guide you to confidently prepare, plan, and execute rituals and ceremonies for all circumstances. This engaging read is perfect for those of you just beginning to recognize and explore your spiritual path, all the way up to the most seasoned and gifted shamans. Whether your occasion is a joyful event such as the birth of a new baby, tough times like transitions, hardships, or endings, or even welcoming nature's changing seasons, the tools are there. Sandra takes her profound insights and knowledge and weaves it all into relevant stories that will lovingly grab you right from page one. The way she meshes new technology with ancient wisdom is brilliant and exciting. While immersing myself in this wondrous work, I experienced a myriad of emotions from laughter to compassionate tears. Keep this book handy. You and your community will visit it often for its simple reminders on how to live life fully as an expression of your gratitude for the unseen world of spirit."

RENEE BARIBEAU
the Practical Shaman, Wind Whistler, and author of *Winds of Spirit: Ancient Wisdom Tools for Navigating Relationships, Health, and the Divine*

"Accessible, inspirational, and informative, *The Book of Ceremony* should be required reading for anyone wishing to live a deeply spiritual life filled with the magic and joy that happens during and because of sacred ceremony. Whether you are a master teacher or in the process of awakening, and whether working alone or in groups, this book is sure to inspire new ideas. I predict that it will become a well-used, dog-eared friend in my library, as I'm sure it will be in yours."

NICKI SCULLY
author of *Sekhmet: Transformation in the Belly of the Goddess* and *Planetary Healing: Spirit Medicine for Global Transformation*

The / *Book of*
CEREMONY

OTHER BOOKS AND LECTURE PROGRAMS
by Sandra Ingerman

BOOKS

Soul Retrieval: Mending the Fragmented Self (HarperOne, 1991)

Welcome Home: Following Your Soul's Journey Home
(HarperOne, 1993)

A Fall to Grace [fiction] (Moon Tree Rising Productions, 1997)

*Medicine for the Earth: How to Transform Personal
and Environmental Toxins* (Three Rivers Press, 2001)

Shamanic Journeying: A Beginner's Guide
[book and drumming CD] (Sounds True, 2004)

How to Heal Toxic Thoughts: Simple Tools for Personal Transformation
(Sterling, 2007)

Awakening to the Spirit World: The Shamanic Path of Direct Revelation
[book and drumming CD; coauthored with Hank Wesselman]
(Sounds True, 2010)

*The Shaman's Toolkit: Ancient Tools for Shaping the Life
and World You Want to Live In* (Weiser, 2010)

*Walking in Light: The Everyday Empowerment
of a Shamanic Life* (Sounds True, 2015)

Speaking with Nature: Awakening to the Deep Wisdom of the Earth
[coauthored with Llyn Roberts] (Inner Traditions, 2015)

The Hidden Worlds [fiction for young adults; coauthored
with Katherine Wood] (Moon Books, 2018)

The *Book of*
CEREMONY

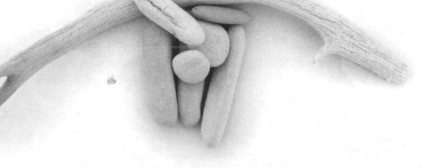

Shamanic Wisdom for
Invoking the Sacred in Everyday Life

SANDRA
INGERMAN

SOUNDS TRUE
BOULDER, COLORADO

Sounds True
Boulder, CO 80306

The wood used to produce this book is from Forest Stewardship
Council (FSC) certified forests, recycled materials, or controlled
wood.

Published 2018

Cover design by Jennifer Miles
Book design by Beth Skelley
Cover image © Elena Ray; Shutterstock.com

Printed in Canada

Library of Congress Cataloging-in-Publication Data
Names: Ingerman, Sandra, author.
Title: The book of ceremony : Shamanic wisdom for invoking the sacred
    in everyday life / Sandra Ingerman.
Description: Boulder, CO : Sounds True, Inc., 2018. |
    Includes bibliographical references.
Identifiers: LCCN 2018004995 (print) | LCCN 2018023184 (ebook) |
    ISBN 9781683641506 (ebook) | ISBN 9781683641490 (pbk.)
Subjects: LCSH: Shamanism. | Rites and ceremonies.
Classification: LCC BF1611 (ebook) | LCC BF1611 .I539 2018 (print) |
    DDC 201/.44—dc23
LC record available at https://lccn.loc.gov/2018004995

10 9 8 7

In love and honor for all the exquisite nature beings in the web of life and to our beautiful Earth.

In deep gratitude for all who keep diving deeper into ceremonial work to return health to all of life and our planet. May our descendants and all in the web of life benefit from our dedicated ceremonial work.

CONTENTS

INTRODUCTION

I love performing ceremonies. I like to perform ceremonies on my own, and I am also passionate about joining with like-minded souls to perform ceremonies for all of life and the Earth.

When I lived in San Francisco in 1980, I was introduced to the practice of shamanic journeying. I loved this practice, which taught me how to receive my own spiritual guidance by traveling outside of time and space to meet with helping and compassionate spirits.

In shamanic teachings, every spiritual and sacred act we perform is a ceremony. When we recognize the sacredness of each moment, miracles happen. In the early 1980s, as I explored the many facets of shamanism, I was drawn to creating shamanic ceremonies to heal my past and to manifest what my soul desired. I knew performing ceremonies was a classic part of shamanic practice.

In the practice of shamanism, the practitioner gazes beyond only what we can see, hear, feel, taste, and smell in our tangible world. Shamans look into the unseen realms, which are filled with great beauty and spiritual healing energies that can empower our lives in ordinary reality.

Using the ancient power of ceremony, shamans move beyond ordinary thinking. And working beyond the tangible world, shamans see disharmonious energetic patterns that need to be rebalanced to improve people's health and the health of the planet. By receiving guidance from the helping spirits, shamans learn to restore harmonious energies through the mysterious healing power of ceremony. Every shamanic journey a shaman takes, every healing method a shaman works with, is considered a ceremony.

Shamanism is a practice of direct revelation. This means shamans receive guidance from their own inner wisdom, communicating with multiple helping and compassionate spirits, and through their deep connection with everything that exists in nature.

In our modern world, we have become so focused on accumulating material wealth and objects, believing this will make us feel whole and joyous. But when you bridge spiritual practices and ceremony into your life, you end up thriving in a more complete way. You live your life with a gleam in your eye as you start to perceive, digest, and absorb more beauty and potential in the world around you, and to understand how you can be an active participant in bringing the sacred into your life.

So many people feel that life is empty and that the outer world holds no meaning. And when we only focus on the tangible realm, that is true. For true joy, wealth, and healing awaits as we learn how to interact with the power of the invisible worlds. Bringing ceremonial practices into our life helps us create a new reality, one filled with richness and purpose as we weave in vibrant energetic threads from the invisible realms. These practices help us find meaning in life and assist us in acknowledging our creative potential.

I performed my first formal shamanic ceremony in 1982—and shortly after that, I moved to Santa Fe, New Mexico. For my ceremony, I first closed the curtains in my living room to darken it, leaving my ordinary thoughts behind and stepping into the mysterious role of the shaman who "sees" in the dark. I still remember the smell of the match when I lit my red candle to begin.

I had a beautiful blanket that was woven with rainbow-colored threads. It felt like a perfect place to create my altar. (Later, while performing healing work, I would ask my clients to lie on this blanket, which I called "my magic carpet into the unseen realms.") I placed an abalone shell filled with the cleansing herbs sage and juniper on my altar. In some traditions, the abalone shell represents the element of water, the cleansing herbs are used as the earth, the match as fire, and the smoke as air. Working with the elements is a way of honoring them for giving us life. Then I placed an offering of red roses on my altar as a gift to the helping spirits who would listen and help me to manifest my prayer.

When I lit the incense, the smoke was filled with a lovely fragrance that felt cleansing on all levels. The glow of the red candle filled the room. The candle's light and the sacred objects on my altar shifted the energy in my living room from an ordinary living space into a sacred spiritual environment.

I remember drumming and standing by the altar I had made with its lovely offerings to the compassionate spirits and to the directions—all the spiritual forces I wanted to honor. I alternated using my rattles and drum to call in the helping spirits as witnesses as I spoke my intention out loud. I asked the spirits to call into my life a spiritual teacher who could take me deeper into my shamanic path.

I could feel all the hairs standing up on my arms, and my heart felt full. I knew as I sang my song that honored all the helping spirits that something big was about to happen. I allowed my spiritual song to emerge, assisting in shifting my ordinary state of consciousness into a shamanic state of consciousness, where I was now ready to engage in sacred ceremonial work.

As I performed each step of the ceremony, my mental chatter about my life dissolved. I stopped worrying about everyday matters like cooking, daily tasks, or news I found disturbing. The more I left my human concerns behind, the more I engaged in the true magic of ceremony.

I wrote my intention on a piece of paper, and once I was ready, I put it into the abalone shell with the burning healing herbs. I lit the paper on fire. This is a symbolic act associated with all fire ceremonies, where you place your intention in the fire, and the smoke carries your desire to the power of the universe that joins with you as a spiritual partner to create your dream or to bring through healing energies.

I thought I was calling in a human teacher. Little did I know that I was actually calling into my life a spiritual teacher from the unseen realms. We don't always know how our intentions might manifest. Over time, I learned that the Spirit of Santa Fe was to become my greatest teacher and would show me how to tap into my creative potential and take my shamanic healing work and teachings into the world.

Over my long history of performing powerful and successful ceremonies, I learned about the elements needed to create such sacred events.

During the 1980s, I began by leading ceremonies in workshops for healing ourselves or for calling in spiritual support for our personal goals.

In 1990, my ceremonial work with groups took a leap when I started teaching five-day workshops on shamanic healing instead of short weekend trainings. During these longer trainings, I led ceremonies for large groups. The ceremonies flowed so smoothly, and these large groups gravitated so strongly to ceremonial work. I could easily see why ceremonies have been performed for thousands of years. Tens of thousands of students have participated in ceremonies I've created. Over the years, participants have given me feedback on not just the power of the ceremony itself, but they have also told me that to bond with community in such an intimate way had created healing beyond the ceremonial work. The community aspect of performing ceremonies gives people an experience they never imagined, bringing comfort, love, and support. Over time, I learned how to bring more power into a ceremony. For example, when performing ceremonies outside, I learned that if I greeted and welcomed the helping ancestors of the land, severe weather and other issues that would have prevented our ceremonial work from taking place would be resolved.

I learned how to help people focus their attention and not drift away during sacred work, because in our culture, most people have short attention spans. I needed to create short ceremonies, or people would lose concentration and would not remember the steps of the ceremony and the intention that went with each phase.

I discovered that ceremony has great power to heal and create positive transformations, but there is also a right timing when desired outcomes will manifest. I had to learn about trust and surrender in performing ceremonies, and I have had to teach my students the same.

There is a lot you can learn from watching and participating in ceremonies. While you can read books and take classes on performing ceremonies, and there are shamanic ways of working that are definitely teachable, be aware that too much focus on acquiring knowledge can keep you in your head instead of helping you move into a life-changing, spiritual state of consciousness and can keep you from seeing through your own eyes. Relying on authority figures disempowers you and diminishes your trust in your own spiritual guidance.

When we attempt to define ancient teachings that focus on energetic work, we disassemble the magic of ceremony. The key, instead, is to unlock your intuitive knowing that invites the power, vibration, and frequency of words and phrases, transforming the results of your ceremony.

As I will continue to share throughout *The Book of Ceremony*, the true positive results come from your desired intention that is heartfelt and authentic, how you honor yourself and the helping spirits, your ability to focus and concentrate as well as create and hold sacred space, and trust in your own intuitive knowing. The success of your ceremonies will evolve over time as you learn how to open your heart to the power of the universe, craft clear intentions, and let go of the outcome.

With ceremonial work, we create sacred space and incubate conscious intentions. We allow the twists and turns, the focus, the willingness to open our hearts and minds. And when ready, we invite other community members into our circle. Afterward, the effects may still be building, so we need to avoid wanting to see immediate results—although immediate results can happen.

The practice of shamanism is not frivolous, nor is it a hobby. For tens of thousands of years, this has been a serious and dignified practice based on helping the community survive. There is a celebratory and often joyous aspect to the work, but there is a difference between being celebratory and being shallow. The practice of shamanism is anything but shallow. If ceremonies for healing, blessing, and divining food sources did not produce good results, people in the community died.

Today, shamanic ceremonies are being used to improve our health and quality of life. But we do need to practice ceremony in a disciplined way. We are witnessing so much devastation in the world, and performing shamanic ceremonies is once again needed for our survival. If we do not take the work seriously, we will lose the power of ceremony that kept our ancestors alive for thousands of years.

Many people still travel to indigenous cultures to learn ceremonies that have been passed down through the generations, and it is quite wonderful to witness these ceremonies, but my interest has been to design ceremonies to meet the current issues we all face living in a modern world. I am devoted to bridging ancient shamanic practices with our modern culture, making them applicable to the issues we face today.

In the last few years, my work has evolved to leading powerful virtual ceremonies in which groups of people from around the world gather in the unseen realms to perform ceremonies of healing and blessings for the group and for the planet.

How to Work with This Book

In *The Book of Ceremony*, I share with you what I have learned over the years, and I hope to inspire you with the many ways you can lead healing and blessing ceremonies. This work is meant to serve your personal healing and growth, and to also be shared with loved ones, friends, coworkers, and eventually with the community you live in.

As my work with ceremony evolved, I was invited to work with diverse communities that had different spiritual and religious beliefs. I found that people will dive in and participate fully in performing a ceremony if the work is explained in an accessible way. We need to use vocabulary that opens people up to the power of love and support without burdening anyone or pushing them away with shamanic principles or terminology that prevent them from engaging fully.

The Book of Ceremony is written for practitioners of shamanism as well as those who have no experience with the practice. With ceremonial work, the key is being willing to open your heart and pray for yourself and others. The helping spirits, the power of the universe, God, the goddess, or whatever numinous spiritual forces you believe in are waiting to help create healing, transformation, and positive change in all our lives and for the Earth. The ceremonies shared can also empower any social activism work you are engaged in.

I also include ceremonies for more experienced shamanic practitioners. As you read the book and work with material on your own, you will know which ceremonies you wish to engage in (or adapt to fit your needs) and which ceremonies hold no interest for you.

Although the ceremonies in the book are not advanced, one could argue about what an "advanced" ceremony is. The truth is that we are facing multiple challenges on the planet. By performing simple ceremonies, we can dissolve collective negative energies such as hate and fear. We do this by engaging our own divine energy and partnering with the divine in the nonordinary realms.

At a time when people are looking for more advanced ceremonies to perform, we need to step back and perform ceremonies that help us to discover who we are as humans and to treat all of life with respect and honor. Destabilizing changes propel us into a higher state of consciousness, which can be attained more gracefully through ceremonial work.

The Book of Ceremony was written to guide you in adapting the ancient art of using ceremony for healing and creating your soul's desires. Please note that the helping spirits will work as partners *with* you—they will not do your personal work *for* you. Spiritual work must be integrated into each person's daily life. It is not enough to perform a beautiful ceremony to create peace. You must commit to your own work to create a landscape of peace within yourself and express peace in your daily actions and choices.

For example, throughout the book I will speak about "expressing," "sending," "transmuting," and "transforming." (I use the words "transmute" and "transform" interchangeably.) We were born to have the full experience of being human. It is critical for our health and well-being to express our feelings, from the joyful states we feel to our feelings of fear, anger, and hate.

At the same time, we don't want to send negative energies into the world to feed more disharmonious states. In the practice of shamanism, we teach the importance of honoring our feelings and expressing them in a healthy way to ourselves and others. Then the next step is to transmute or transform the energy behind our emotions into energies of love and light that feed us and the planet with healthy, harmonious, loving, and peaceful energies. The energies we feed are the ones that grow.

Think of expressing your feelings as discharging some of the challenging energy you are holding in your body. Hold the intention of asking your inner divine to transform the energy you are feeling to a nourishing vibration of love and light radiating throughout the entire web of life. I do this by repeating a prayer: "May all the energy behind my negative emotions be transformed to love and light."

In the chapters that follow, I share how to perform ceremonies to release an emotional block or hurt into the elements of earth, air, water, or fire. Please remember to repeat a prayer like the one shared here so that all is transformed into loving and light-filled energies nurturing life.

I will continue to encourage you to leave your ordinary and burdening thoughts behind, so you are not anchored to this ordinary realm while performing your ceremonies. Please understand that I am not asking you to deny your feelings. I share a lot of tools on how to transform your energy in my book *Walking in Light: The Everyday Empowerment of a Shamanic Life*.

I am passionate about creating a strong, spiritual global community. Throughout the book, I invite you into the global community that is joining together to be in service to all of life and the Earth.

I tend to use gardening terms as a metaphor for our inner and outer life. We must plant the seeds in our inner and outer life that we want to see grow, cultivate our dreams, and harvest the plants from the result of our ceremonial work. With our intentions for our ceremonies, we plant spiritual seeds in our inner landscape—the garden that lives within us. And what we feed, grows.

When we perform ceremonies, we are immersed in nature's cycles of exploring the shadow and the light, death and rebirth. This is necessary for us to attune to our nature and how we grow, evolve, transform, and heal.

Many today are working with ceremony to acknowledge the spirit of the land they live on and the trees, plants, animals, and other life-forms that live in their locale. Groups of people are gathering to perform ceremonies welcoming new seasons and honoring the change in the phases of the moon. This helps us reconnect with nature, bringing a deeper relationship with the land we live on, and a return to emotional and physical health and balance.

Ceremonies are being performed to support a move and bless a new house or apartment. In this way, we establish a harmonious relationship with the home we live in, creating a feeling of comfort and safety. People connect with the power of the universe to help find a new job, creating more meaningful work—not just a job that supports pure financial survival. Ceremonies are used to bless changes and transitions in life.

People are turning to ceremonies to ask for a positive outcome when moving through life changes, to honor the environment, and to ask for help during extreme climate changes.

More people are willing to introduce loved ones, friends, and coworkers to ceremonies to be performed together to create stronger and healthier relationships.

Through opening our hearts to all the possibilities that life has to offer and being willing to stretch our imaginations, we find that there are a wealth of ceremonies we can use to unburden ourselves from our past hurts, traumas, and self-sabotaging beliefs, moving us into a place where we feel a deeper relationship with life and why we are here.

We will still face challenges in our work, and these experiences help us grow toward our authentic natures. Being part of the status quo is not why we are here. We are here to manifest our passions and to grow. We need to stretch beyond the limiting beliefs that society places on us.

Today, many alternative healing traditions teach about neuroplasticity. This scientific knowledge shows how flexible the brain is and how we can create new neuropathways through positive thinking to help us recover from emotional and physical illnesses.

Shamans were the first people to teach about neuroplasticity. But they did not teach about positive thinking. Instead, they taught that the words, thoughts, and daydreams we focus on throughout the day can either bless or curse us and others.

One way to work with neuroplasticity is to maintain a state of gratitude and positive thoughts, feelings, and memories. We give attention to what is working in our lives instead of what does not work. We are encouraged to use our imagination to help the brain manifest a state of physical and emotional well-being. Working with gratitude and holding a positive vision are key principles in living shamanism as a way of life.

When we perform ceremonies, we transform the negative thoughts and states of consciousness burdening us. We can then use ceremony to ground and manifest the thoughts and dreams we do want to create in our life. Ceremony impacts us deeply on a subconscious level, creating positive change.

In the world of shamanism, everything that exists on the planet is connected to a web of life as one living organism. You can think of this web like your body. You are made up of multiple organs and cells, each of which affects your health, and each of which is impacted by your words, thoughts, and energy. In the same way, the web of life is a weaving of living creatures who all contribute to, are impacted by, and are energetically reshaped by our intentions, thoughts, words, daydreams, and states of consciousness. You can create positive outcomes for all in the web of life by bringing the sacred into your everyday life with ceremony. If you perform one powerful and successful ceremony for yourself, the principle of oneness ensures that all of life heals and evolves from the work you did. For all of life is connected—and in shamanism, where unity consciousness pervades the work, all minds are connected.

Despite the appearance of separation and conflict, we face the deeper truth that we are part of an interconnected web of life. This connects us to the matrix of life itself. Although we all have a unique energetic signature, we are part of one living, breathing organism.

You will learn specific details about designing ceremonies in *The Book of Ceremony*. I offer examples of many types of ceremonies that I, my students, or my peers have designed, participated in, witnessed, or heard about. I have changed some of the details to respect the privacy of the people involved. Let these examples stimulate your imagination to design ceremonies that speak to your needs and the needs of your community. By developing your own unique ceremonies, you bring a freshness and aliveness into your ceremonial work, fueling the power of the results of your work.

In the practice of shamanism, every word, thought, and daydream is an energetic vibration that can be sculpted into form. In the universe, there is mostly formlessness. In shamanism, we can work with formless energies such as love, light, and peace. Through ceremony, we work to mold into form the powerful energies we want to witness in our lives and on the planet.

The big challenge in our culture in performing ceremonial work is to put down our devices, move hectic thoughts out of the way, and think for ourselves. The helping spirits work with us in partnership as a team. As part of this team, everyone must commit to the job of holding the space and letting the steps of the ceremony arise from our heart.

I have defined certain terms that might cause some initial confusion. But it is important to remember that what shamans experience in their ceremonial work is beyond what we can see in our tangible world. When we try to rigidly define certain teachings and terms in shamanism, we can lose the true meaning as it touches us on a soul level. Spirit is not meant to be understood by the mind. If you find that there is a term or word that you do not understand, close your eyes and imagine traveling inside yourself to where your intuition and inner wisdom are. Try to get a sense of the term or word on a feeling level rather than trying to rationally understand it.

The key of the power of shamanism is that it is a system of direct revelation. Shamanism relies on you being able to wake up your intuitive knowing rather than rationally trying to define the deep and magical mysteries of life. When you allow teachers to give you too much rational information, you stay on the surface waves of the work. Successful ceremonial work requires that you dive deeper. From a shamanic point of view, your health and the health of the planet is dependent on serious ceremonial work.

When you were born, you came into the world with an energetic signature that holds the energy of unique gifts you came to share in some way to assist in keeping the web of life strong. When we give our power away to other authorities, the gifts we were born to contribute cannot emerge. Many in today's world do not trust themselves or do not feel worthy, so they turn to others to tell them what to do.

Of course, seeking guidance from experienced practitioners is necessary from time to time. But remember, there are amazing insights waiting for you to discover if you recognize that you are a unique being born with a wealth of inner wisdom and presence to share with the web of life. We all lose something when you do not trust yourself and shine. Trust yourself.

For everyone reading *The Book of Ceremony*, I share guidance, not rules. I guide you from my personal experience leading ceremonies and teaching others how to design ceremonies that can be performed solo or in a group. Just by performing ceremonies, you will find yourself stepping into a beautiful and creative power you might not yet have imagined.

As you greet and welcome your helping spirits to perform a powerful and successful ceremony, keep an open mind to the many ways unique and remarkable compassionate spirits can show up to help you. Over time, you will come to depend on them to perform still deeper ceremonial work.

As you continue your ceremonial work, it will organically deepen. No one can teach you how to deepen your ceremonial work—it happens through experience. Over time, you will reshape the wording of your intentions, invocations, prayers, and songs. Even some shamans in indigenous cultures are evolving their songs to shift the disharmonious energies they are facing in the current times.

One of my students wrote, "Words are so powerful, and when selected through meditation, they sharpen the thought to a powerful point."

Through practice, you will naturally find that your new words and songs manifest higher frequencies that organically intensify and empower your work. Your work will become more potent as you awaken your inner spiritual fire and your connection to divine forces. I know this sounds counterintuitive, but going deeper is a passive process. If you try too hard, you may stay in the shallow waters through overthinking instead of trusting spirit.

Only practice and experience can be your teacher. Keep going deeper, and the rewards for yourself and the planet will be great!

If a ceremony I describe calls to you and feels like it would help improve the quality of your life or others, use it as is. You might find as you continue your ceremonial work that the greatest power in your ceremonies occurs when you drop into your heart and soul, allowing your ceremony to flow with ease and grace.

There may be times when it isn't appropriate to follow the guidelines of a ceremony exactly as I describe it. For example, if you just experienced a big trauma in your life, you are at the scene of an accident, or during a natural disaster, you might not want to get out instruments, prepare, and design a ceremony to do. You might just drop to your knees and ask the helping spirits or the divine for help. Or you might bury and honor a bird, a snake, or another animal that was killed on the road. This is a ceremony too.

Teaching people how to design and perform ceremonies is a joy for me. Performing ceremonies alone or with groups lights up my eyes, and I feel so much bliss, love, and light pulsing through me. I feel regenerated and alive, connected with nature and the forces of the universe that support our growth and evolution.

It is an extraordinary feeling when I prepare to perform a ceremony in solitude, or with a group meeting together in the physical, or even a virtual ceremony in which the group meets in the unseen realms. My heart expands while I gather my needed tools and supplies. Once ready to welcome and greet the helping spirits, I feel excitement. And when I state my intention and then follow through on the steps of the ceremony, I feel a deep connection with a force much greater than myself.

I hope that as you read on and perform your ceremonies you will have your own heart-opening experiences that bring joy and meaning into your life. Even when performing a ceremony to release a wound, creating a deep sadness and tears, there is such a sense of connection to a spiritual force that loves you and supports your work.

I envision that once you start performing your own ceremonies, you will reach out to share this empowering work with others. We are hungry to connect with more than just what we experience with our ordinary senses in the material world. There is a desire to bond together with others to receive support and unconditional love as we step forward on our path of healing and evolution.

After a student of mine got the courage to share a ceremony in her community, a participant said, "You had no right to keep such important work from us." She meant that everyone was so grateful that she had reached deep inside to find the courage to share the transformation that occurs for others while performing a ceremony.

As I write this book on ceremony, I reflect on the ceremonies I've performed in the past. I often think joyfully of being in community, drumming, rattling, singing, dancing, and entering an ecstatic state of consciousness in communion with the helping spirits, nature, and others who are like-minded, all focusing on the intention of supporting each other during our healing and transitions. These experiences are tied to the most marvelous, most precious, and happiest memories I have about my life. I have equally beautiful memories about the quieter and heart-expanding ceremonies I have led to help family and loved ones honor the transition of someone who has died, or drumming and holding space for someone who buries a wedding ring after a divorce.

Storms on all levels of life impact us as they are part of nature's cycles. Performing ceremonies helps us navigate the turbulent waves and builds up the spiritual strength to ride the challenging waves of any crisis. And when we gather together in community during times of crisis, we have a community "Spirit Boat" to help carry us through any challenge.

May your ceremonies open you up to the joy of partnering with community and the helping spirits. May the work bring you a sense of empowerment and bring the healing and blessings you so deserve.

We all deserve the goodness that life has to offer. I hope you reflect later in your life on the exquisite nature of performing ceremonial work. Every moment in life and every living being is sacred. When we recognize this, we create magic and joy in our lives.

Part One

THE POWER OF CEREMONY

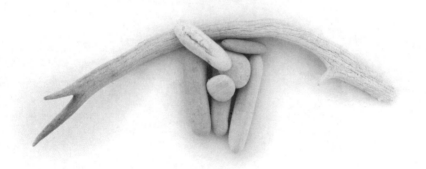

WHAT CEREMONY IS

Ceremony brings the sacred into ordinary life. For tens of thousands of years, ceremonies have been universally used to help communities navigate change and welcome in new cycles. Performing ceremonies creates a bridge between the material world we live in and the world of the unseen, the divine, the power of the universe. In modern terms, ceremony opens a phone line between you and the power of the universe, God, the goddess, the Creator. Through this line of connection, you can have direct communication between yourself and spiritual forces, creating a partnership to manifest your desired outcome.

In shamanic cultures, a variety of creation stories teach how life and the Earth was formed. Stories range from a variety of gods and goddesses, as well as the creative forces of the universe, manifesting life-forms and the planet Earth out of unconditional love. Some creation myths share how Grandmother Spider weaved the world into being, and some speak to the metaphor of the Creator sculpting life and the Earth into form as one would mold clay. There are a wealth of stories about how the vibration of the energy of words created the world of form. Creation stories were reenacted and honored through ceremony.

Many ancient cultures share the insight that this world is a dream and an illusion. We are given a role to play in life, and part of that role is to learn how to mold spirit into form just like the Creator or creative forces of the universe did billions of years ago.

In the shamanic understanding, the world of form we see, hear, touch, smell, and taste starts as vibrations in the invisible and transcendent realms. Through words and thought forms, these vibrations transition from the transcendent realm and manifest on the Earth and in the world of physical form. For shamans, the world is seen as a dream, and we are active participants in creating the dream through our words and thoughts. This dream ends up creating the reality we live in for ourselves and for all life on Earth.

Think of the vibration of our thoughts and words spinning together just like a spinner spins fiber, and then the fibers weave together to create the fabric of reality we now live in. The vibrations of our thoughts and words create strong, resonant waves throughout the universe that change the course of our lives and that of the planet. Your view of yourself, others, and the world is made of thoughts that weave together to create the fabric of your life. Everything in the universe is seen as energy that can manifest into form over time through our intention. And using ceremony is a powerful tool to create and transform the world of form.

In shamanic cultures, the shaman and the community members actively engage in the role of creating a good life for all in the community. Much of the work they do to ensure harmonious connections with life, nature, and others is through the power of ceremony.

Working together with the compassionate spirits and the divine, the shaman and the community state their intention, which spins threads through the invisible collective energy fields to call in blessings and healing for the community. By opening to the power of love, stating a strong intention, and staying focused and fully engaged during the ceremony, they generate a powerful collective field of energy where the threads of creation can manifest into form.

The Practice of Shamanism and Ceremonial Work

The practice of shamanism is a universal practice that is tens of thousands of years old. The compassionate helping spirits gave our ancestors the practice of shamanism to help them survive. The helping spirits gifted the human race with this practice for divining information, healing emotional and physical illness, and connecting with our environment. This work has always been honored, and experienced shamanic teachers around the planet are helping to carry this precious gift into the world, so all people can receive the blessing of the work.

In the ethnographic literature, a shaman is defined as a man or woman who journeys into the invisible realms, also called nonordinary reality, the unseen realms, the Dreamtime, and the Other World as well as other terms to describe another dimension of reality. In the unseen transcendent realms, there is a wealth of helping and compassionate spirits who volunteer themselves to shamans and the rest of humanity to share guidance about practical details, such as how to live a healthy and empowered life and when and how to perform healing, blessing, and initiation ceremonies. We all have access to these helping and compassionate spirits to guide us.

Shamans have been and are still seen as "ones who know." They bridge the physical realm and realms of spirit to bring balance to the community and heal the sick. Shamans are healers, mystics, prophets, and seers. They have always traveled into the invisible realms to bring back the gift of healing.

We live in a time when many people are waking up to the shamanic understanding that everything that exists is alive. There is more to the reality we live in then just how our senses engage with the tangible world—what we see, hear, feel, taste, and smell in this ordinary realm. Once we wake up and recognize that other spectacular dimensions of reality exist, we experience a new sense of awareness about how to connect with nature, the flow of life, and the web of life. We come to realize that we have the power to connect to life in a whole new way that creates positive changes in our own life and for all of life. We then take on the gift of the shaman as one who can see into dimensions beyond the ordinary world we live in.

Shamans help the community stay connected to the web of life by speaking to "the spirit that lives in all things." Shamans have always spoken to the wind, the rain, the sun, the earth, the mountains, the sea, the clouds, the planets, the stars, the moon, and all the energies that affect us daily. By doing this, shamans watch for the signs of change. They can know when to perform ceremonies to honor rites of passage and initiation, when to plant crops, when to hunt, and when to honor the elements so that the community can live in harmony with the change of seasons, the lunar cycles, and nature's flow.

Shamans might receive a sign that it is time to perform a ceremony by watching how the constellations appear in the night sky, tracking the phase of the moon, observing the movement of the clouds, or by opening their invisible ears to listen to messages brought by the wind.

Shamans may sit gazing around the fire at night for hours to receive visions. A shaman can notice a change coming by observing shifting behavior of the wind, animals, and birds. Or a shaman might speak to a tree or plant to receive a message that appears as a symbol, a sensed feeling, or a telepathic message informing the shaman when and how to perform a ceremony.

Shamans and people living in traditional cultures are taught from birth how to open their invisible senses of sight, hearing, smell, touch, and taste so that communicating with all of nature is as natural an act as turning to a friend and having a conversation. When people in shamanic cultures walk through nature, they walk listening and seeing with their entire body. They do not depend on their ordinary eyes and ears. Their entire body provides guidance. We all have the ability to speak to the spirit of all the nature beings as well as to the elements (earth, air, water, and fire) that give us life. We just need to wake up and acknowledge our invisible senses and connections. When we deaden our senses, we miss so much ever-present beauty and guidance that nature provides.

The shaman or someone else in the community might have a prophetic dream about a challenge coming that could be avoided by performing the appropriate ceremony. Good omens can appear in dreams to signal when it's time to welcome a new stage of life or take action to bring the goodness of life to a community. Community members in many traditional cultures often meet first thing in the morning to share their dreams so that the information they've gathered on challenges and good times can be worked with through ceremony.

The shaman, with other members of the community, might ingest a psychoactive plant that grows on their land and receive visions about blessing or healing ceremonies needed to serve the community.

Each cycle and season of life we go through can be honored to help create a smooth transition from one phase to another. Blessing ceremonies allow us to greet the sun each day; to greet and give thanks to the elements earth, air, water, and fire; to welcome in all changes and transitions we go through in life; and to grieve the variety of losses we experience as humans. We can welcome children into the world through blessing ceremonies. And when we need help to reestablish harmony, we can perform a healing ceremony to remove negative energy, to restate an intention, and finally to ask for blessings for the dreams and desires of the community.

Healing ceremonies are performed to retrieve lost power and a lost soul, extract an illness, or remove a possessing spirit. Shamans perform ceremonies to heal ancestral issues. A good, harmonious relationship with our ancestors is important in maintaining physical and emotional health. Ceremonies can help us break old karmic patterns that we might be reenacting from another lifetime.

Ceremonies are also used to honor and give thanks to the helping and compassionate spirits who provide a wealth of assistance and heal-ing. When we perform a ceremony, we create a strong link with the helping spirits and the power of the universe that work in partnership with us to assist in manifesting desired outcomes. Once you develop a strong relationship with the helping spirits, the Creator, and your own divine Self, you can be the sculptor of your life.

By performing ceremonies, change happens. As we call in our desires and release our blocks, we are free to step into a new dimen-sion of life where we can feel the unlimited potential of what we can create during our lifetime.

We cannot through science, technology, or even with our rational mind disconnect from the cycles and initiations of life. For we are living beings who are ruled by nature, not by our mind. As we have lost sight of the spiritual power of ceremony, we have created a life and a world where we live as if we are separate from nature. We hold the false belief that we can control the changes in our life. Many of us resist change. In turning away from our connection to a larger force and a bigger picture, we disconnect from the flow of life.

By bringing ceremony into our life, we reconnect with the sacred as we move from a state of disconnection to a state of reconnection to life and nature. We begin to intentionally work with the threads we spin in the invisible realms that weave into forms that impact all in the web of life.

Ceremony creates change and is transformative in itself, while supporting a sense of greater ease as we experience the transitions of life. Through ceremony, we reestablish a healthy and powerful relationship to nature. One of the guiding teachings in shamanism is the principle of reciprocity. If you honor and respect life and reestablish your connection with nature, the helping spirits and nature will honor you in return.

The Difference Between Ceremony and Ritual

A common question that emerges for people is "What is the difference between ritual and ceremony?" I will give you my definition, and over time, you might find your own way of perceiving the difference.

When I get up every day and immediately stand and give thanks to the sun for bringing the energy to thrive, I consider this a ritual. If I organize my ritual where I start to sing and drum and do the preparation as described later in this book, that would be a ceremony. Ritual work is work that will be repeated daily, once a week, or once a month.

A ceremony is performed to ask for a specific outcome, and although it might need to be repeated, it tends to be performed at a specific time for a specific intention. Many people perform the same ritual on a regular basis, whereas a ceremony changes over time.

For example, research shows that walking through a forest and doing what is called "forest bathing" brings about wellness due to the healing organic compounds the forest emits. If I perform forest bathing daily, that is a ritual. If I design a shamanic event to honor the trees that bring healing to me, that is a ceremony.

CEREMONY TODAY

There is a huge resurgence occurring in the practice of shamanism in the Western world as people search for ways to improve the quality of their lives and to be in service to the Earth. If you're just beginning to step into the magical world of performing ceremonies, you may feel fearful about performing a ceremony incorrectly and bringing harm into your life. We did not grow up in a family system or society where the power of working in the invisible realms was recognized. Working with ceremony is often left to religious services, where there can be a lot of dogma involved that obscures the joyful dance we can do with the universe to help heal ourselves and the planet.

Don't worry about what is "correct" or "incorrect" with designing your sacred work. Once you perform ceremonies and see the joy and freedom from linking with the creative forces of the universe, you'll learn to relax into the dance between humans and compassionate spirits that creates true transformation. With each ceremony, you'll move a little deeper into the Great Mystery, and you'll open your heart and imagination to design ceremonies that will support your path.

The Book of Ceremony is written for a variety of readers—for those trained in shamanic work as well as for a nonshamanic audience. If you do not engage in the practice of shamanic journeying, simply interpret references to "helping and compassionate spirits" to mean any divine force you believe in.

After reading *The Book of Ceremony*, if you find you would like to learn the practice of shamanic journeying and connecting with helping and compassionate spirits, I provide a list of books, audio programs, and online courses that will teach you the practice in the resources section at the end of this book.

Children are true masters at creating ceremony. The veils between the visible and invisible have yet to close for children as they have in adults. If you ask your child or the children in your community to create a ceremony, you will be amazed by how their ceremonies are filled with love and joy. They will help you decorate the ceremonial space, advise everyone on what to wear, and assist in creating a perfectly orchestrated ceremony. Even if you do not ask a child to help you design a ceremony, invite any child who would like to attend. The impact on them will be great. They will be inspired and feel more hopeful about their own life and the future.

THE EXPONENTIAL POWER OF WORKING IN A GROUP

Many of us, including myself, like to engage in private ceremonial work. These ceremonies let us sit in nature, meditate, and reflect. They let us walk, drum, rattle, dance, chant our prayers and sing our songs of gratitude, and receive guidance while communing with the elements and helping spirits.

However, the power generated is exponentially greater when we perform ceremonies in a group. For more than thirty-five years, I have been teaching practitioners how to perform healing ceremonies. I have witnessed time and again how much more powerful a ceremony is when a group participates instead of a lone practitioner performing the ceremony for a client. I've also seen this amplification when performing ceremonies on behalf of the planet.

There is a rise in destruction occurring from climate change, violence, and challenging planetary issues impacting all of life. When we gather as a community to perform ceremonies, positive change does happen. We begin building a world of invisible substance. In all healing—whether it is personal healing or global healing—something first happens on an invisible level before you actually see the results of it in the physical world. When everyone in a group or community works together at the invisible level first, the result can lead to powerful transformational change to create a healthier world.

WORKING IN COLLECTIVE FIELDS OF ENERGY

When people work together in a physical or virtual ceremony, the group generates a field of energy. It is especially important that everyone do their preparation work, as I will describe in chapter 3, to spiritually cleanse and leave their ordinary day and concerns behind.

You want the field you are stepping into to be clear, pristine, and filled with love and light. When people perform ceremonies and truly open their hearts and minds to the unseen worlds, they become psychically sensitive and vulnerable to negative energies from others in the group.

I was with a group in Denali National Park in Alaska once, far out in the wilderness. There were no phone lines, TVs, electrical lines. There was just pure, clean air to breathe and no distracting energies to prevent anyone's energy field from expanding as fully as possible, allowing us to dive deeply into our spiritual work. There were no negative energies to clear, as the land was untouched. This is just an example of the energy and sacred space we want to create in our ceremonial work. Many of us live in cities with distractions that don't exist in the wilderness. But we want to create that same kind of clear, holy, sacred space so that everyone who enters leaves the ceremonial work feeling regenerated.

It is the role of the leader of the group as well as the participants to make sure the field is clear so that true, pristine sacred space is created. It is also the role of the leader to hold space and be an energetic anchor for the group by staying centered. Some people are gifted at holding space and keeping the energy of the ceremony centered, grounded, and filled with peace, love, and grace.

WORKING FROM YOUR SPIRITUAL HEART

While I was writing *The Book of Ceremony*, there were a lot of catastrophic events occurring on the planet. Hopefully, those in future generations will benefit from the deep ceremonial work people around the world have been performing to help heal the destructive energies on the planet. But due to watching so many beings suffer, many people have moved into a place of hopelessness.

One of my spiritual teachers in the unseen realms is the Egyptian goddess Isis. She shared a powerful message to help people experience a deeper place from which to perform ceremonial work. Her message really spoke to me and helped me deepen my own work. I hope it is inspiring to you too.

Here is what Isis shared:

> Here on Earth, you were born to experience love, light, and joy. But the lesson is to first experience suffering, and then to reach beyond suffering to the place inside of you (not outside of you) of love and spiritual bliss.
>
> So many are experiencing and seeing suffering. On an evolutionary level, this is expanding your sense of compassion. It takes you deep into your humanness. But if you are still trapped in the energy, vibration, frequency of suffering, you will carry that energy in your body and project it to the world. By carrying the energy of suffering, many people are becoming ill.
>
> You are now literally and metaphorically being cracked open to the deepest place of your humanness within, where all the knowledge and wisdom is waiting for you to learn.
>
> In your world, you are encouraged to open your heart to the spirit of love. This teaching is not meant to focus on your physical heart, which is simply part of your ego.
>
> Behind your physical heart is a spiritual heart. Your spiritual heart is always close and available when you tune in to it. It is talked about by many gurus, mystics, and spiritual teachers.
>
> And this spiritual heart—one with Source and the joy, bliss, and unconditional love for all of life and creation—knows no suffering. It knows bliss, it knows unconditional love, but it has no experience of suffering on this Earth.
>
> Perform your ceremonial work by radiating light from your spiritual heart. Be a presence of love as your heart emanates pure, nonpersonal, unconditional love.

All ceremonies have a beginning, middle, and end. In the next chapter you will learn about the beginning pieces you can use to start your work so that your ceremony becomes a sacred event.

2

ENVISIONING YOUR CEREMONY

While performing shamanic ceremonies, we open the door between our ordinary consciousness—who we are on an egoic and personality level—and walk through a veil that leads into the invisible realms.

You have to leave behind your ordinary thoughts about your day to cross the veil into the invisible and start your process of weaving a new life tapestry for yourself, your family, your community, and the world. Thinking about emails or what happened at work or concerns about issues in your life anchors you to the ordinary, preventing you from crossing to the unseen world and experiencing the power of the work.

THE TRUE MAGIC BEHIND CEREMONIES

The true magic in working with ceremonies is what occurs behind all the activity taking place. This is true with all shamanic healing and blessing work.

The space behind the drumming, the words, the dancing, and all the physical activity of ceremony is the deep silence of the void—the place before creation. In this silent space, your soul communes with the divine forces and the powers that be, working in partnership to manifest the intention of your ceremony.

The activity of ceremony gives us a way to feed and grow the seed of intention. We focus our body, mind, and spirit, making a path for the magic to occur behind the veil, between the seen and unseen realms.

When a master shaman performs a healing, the true work has nothing to do with the method performed. The healing happens in the sacred space of the void and through the light-filled presence of the shaman.

If you create sacred space, magic happens in your ceremony. You are operating on different levels of reality simultaneously. Your inner divine spirit and the divine power of the universe commune within the structure of the ceremony, allowing you in your humanness to participate and to show your commitment and intention to obtain your desired results.

I will now share with you elements that are essential in designing and preparing for a ceremony that you perform alone or in a group.

CHOOSING THE RIGHT PLACE FOR YOUR CEREMONY

If you are working indoors, you want to find the appropriate room to work in. For example, if you want to work with fire, pick a room where there is a fireplace or a room where you can safely burn something small, like a piece of paper. Use a controlled flame, such as from a candle, and make sure all the ash goes into a bowl.

When your ceremony involves playing an instrument and stating your prayers out loud, find a room in which you will not be disturbed. A phone ringing in the middle of the ceremony might bring you out of sacred space, and you might lose your concentration and focus. If there are other people in the house with whom you feel shy about sharing your work, pick a time of day when you can be alone. Or simply ask everyone to respect your need for privacy.

If you play an instrument or generate positive spiritual power during your ceremony, pets in your house will be attracted and will want to be with you. You have to use your judgment. Having animals to love and support you during a ceremony is a precious thing, but they can be distracting if they get too active or noisy.

My cat would literally throw herself against the door of my office so that I'd let her in when I was performing any kind of ceremony.

Once in the room, she would just lie down and purr. She became a great supporter of my work.

When working outside, find a location where you won't be disturbed by the public. This place needs to feel safe to you. And when you go inside yourself and notice your feelings in this location, you should feel an inner smile or an inner "ah" that says to you, "This is a good place to work."

Be aware that ceremonies generate a lot of good energy. I have taught at retreat centers where other groups are working. They tend to gravitate to the energy of deep and intimate ceremonies. I have gone back and forth on this issue. Sometimes I have explained to strangers showing up that this is an intimate healing ceremony for our group and ask for privacy. But I was at one retreat center where a couple showed up uninvited. They asked if they could keep their distance and just soak in the good, joyful, healing energy. How could I say no? And I've never said no again. This is something for you to decide if you do ceremonies in public places. Of course, if you are performing a ceremony for your community, then all members are welcome.

Once you discover a good place to work, I suggest connecting with the helping ancestral spirits of the land. The compassionate ancestral spirits of the land are human spirits who are now deceased but chose to stay on Earth, rather than returning home to Source, to protect and care for the land they so love. They love the land as much as we do. It is important for them to know the intention of the spiritual work you are doing, as they will support you. They sometimes will even help to create the perfect weather for you to work in.

Leave an offering for the helping ancestral spirits. In many traditional cultures around the world, tobacco and special foods and drink were typically left as offerings. You can leave organic tobacco, lavender, or some herb that has special meaning to you. I leave blue corn meal, which is a sacred plant that has deep meaning to me. Please be aware that animals will eat your offerings, so be sure not to leave out food or drink that might hurt an animal that ingests it.

You will notice that you receive special help with your ceremony when you ask permission of the compassionate ancestors on the land.

When the helping ancestors feel honored, they are always enthusiastic to help.

If you have a particular element in mind that you want to work with (earth, air, water, or fire), then you must find a location in nature where that element exists. For example, if you want to ask the sea to release you from a wound you are carrying, you need to work by the ocean. But if you cannot find the site you need locally, you can easily find a location in the unseen realms. In nonordinary reality, there are beautiful territories you can visit to perform ceremonial work—oceans, forests, waterfalls, rivers, mountains, and anything else you would need.

This is one of the benefits of choosing to work with a spiritual ceremony that includes a journey or meditation into the invisible, nonordinary realms. Another benefit is that it gives you the ability to connect with others over long distances and form circles in the unseen realms. Throughout *The Book of Ceremony*, this way of working remotely will be referred to as "virtual" ceremonies.

There are pros and cons in choosing whether you wish to perform a ceremony inside or outside. When working outside, you get to gaze upon the exquisite elements of nature. If you work with a group and use shamanic instruments such as drums and rattles, the sound gets diffused by the wind and more attention is needed to stay focused. But there is such a power in performing a ceremony outside in nature that most of my students prefer to work outdoors if weather conditions allow it.

People get so much healing from working in nature. It changes their mood, and afterward, their faces shine with light and love.

When you perform a ceremony inside, the energy is more contained and can oftentimes seem more powerful. The drumming, singing, or chanting can get quite loud, so there needs to be a discussion about keeping the volume to a level that supports the work while not becoming a distraction. It is common for one or more people to enter an ecstatic state during a ceremony and not realize how loud they have become. I instruct my students before an indoor ceremony to gently tap on the shoulder of someone who is in a state of ecstasy to lovingly let them know they are being too loud.

CHOOSING A POTENT TIME FOR YOUR CEREMONY

Every day is a good day to perform a ceremony. As I shared in chapter 1, shamans perform ceremonies based on the phases of the moon and where the stars are in the sky, or on the equinox or solstice, or when there is a need for a ceremony. Someone in the community might have a dream that signals a time to perform a ceremony, or the shaman might observe omens in nature that reveal the appropriate time.

If you have a strong need for a healing or a blessing, perform your ceremony when you feel called to do so. If you are welcoming a baby into the world, you want to perform the ceremony close the baby's birth. There are other ceremonies where the timing will be obvious. When performing ceremonies to honor life's changes, choosing to work on the full or new moon, during seasonal changes, or when an initiation or rite of passage is occurring are all good times to do your work. You might prefer to connect with the power of the sun and perform your ceremony at sunrise, dusk, or sunset, or you might prefer to do this work when the moon and stars are shining brightly in the night sky.

As shamanism is a way of life, you can be spontaneous with your ceremonies. You might find yourself out in nature and feel guided to pick up a stick and break it, signifying that you are ready to disconnect from an unhealthy relationship. Or you might be sitting in a beautiful place in nature and decide to use your breath to blow your old wounds into a stone and then bury the stone in the earth, always ending with gratitude for the earth's ability to release the energy as fertilizer for new growth. These spontaneous acts are types of healing ceremony.

GATHERING YOUR MATERIALS

You want to prepare your materials before you perform your ceremony. The flow of your ceremony will not be graceful if you have to stop and search for an object you need.

31

Playing Shamanic and Spiritual Music

Music has a special power to engage us in ceremony, quiet our mind, and dissolve distracting energy. If you're using recorded music, have your track ready to play. You may also decide to use shamanic instruments to help you focus on your work, such as a drum, rattle, flute, Tibetan bowl, click sticks, or bells. If it feels appropriate, you can make rattles by putting stones, crystals, or seeds in a bottle. You can find two sticks and click them together if you do not have a drum.

Drumming has been used universally by shamans for tens of thousands of years. Scientific research has shown that listening to monotonous percussion slows down our brain waves from a beta state, which is our ordinary state of consciousness, to a theta state. The change of consciousness produced by the theta state assists us in traveling from the seen into the unseen realms.

If you are not a shamanic practitioner, you might bring in any instrument or music that will support you staying concentrated on your intention leading to your desired outcome. Be sure your music is always chosen with the intention of creating a sacred space.

Keeping an open heart lets your intentions travel into the power of the universe to be manifested. Listening to music, playing instruments, singing, and dancing are all ways to open your heart and move you out of your rational mind.

Gathering Items in Nature

When collecting items in nature, speak to their spirit before taking them for your altar or ceremonial work. For example, before using lavender as an offering, ask the spirit of lavender if it is okay to pick it. You can do this with all flowers, stones, and crystals you find to work with. Trust your intuition on the answer you receive. The spirit of nature speaks to us all the time. We just need to open our invisible senses to receive images, messages, and feelings.

Using Materials to Design Your Space and Ceremony

There are many ways to use objects in your ceremony. For instance, in preparing an object to burn in a fire ceremony, you might wind yarn around a stick to create an effigy, talisman, or power object that is empowered with your intention for healing or blessing.

If you want to put materials into water or earth for your ceremony, then gather objects from nature beforehand that are safe—such as a beautiful stone that has a shape that calls to you. Prepare by empowering the stone with a prayer that you release into the water or the earth. Or you might take some organic cloth and fill it with sacred herbs, tying it up into a small medicine bundle. Using your breath, you can blow in your intention before releasing it to the element you are working with.

You might use paper to write a letter to a person the ceremony involves, or to God, the goddess, or the power of the universe. You can write a word describing a wish or a quality you wish to release. Or you might draw a symbolic picture. The paper can be burned in a fire ceremony or buried in the earth.

I like to use a wonderful paper called dissolving paper. I have included the website where you can order this in the resources section at the end of the book. You can write on the paper what you wish to release or a blessing you wish to manifest. Then you put the paper in a bowl of warm water and watch it dissolve. The paper is made with materials that are safe for the environment. After the paper has dissolved in the water, you can feed it to the earth. As you can imagine, children love to work with dissolving paper in ceremonies.

Feathers are excellent ceremonial items. You can blow the energy you're releasing into a feather and then shake the energy of your wound into the air, water, earth, or fire while focusing on the released energy being transmuted into light and love that nurtures the Earth and all of life. I do encourage you to know the source of your feathers. Many birds are being killed for their feathers because they are popular to use in ceremony. We want to make sure that we collect our feathers in ways that honor the spirit of the bird. This is true for any animal parts we wear or use in our ceremonial work.

If you are working with a Prayer, Blessing, or Wishing Tree (which I will describe in the chapters that follow), you will want to gather ribbon or yarn or make prayer ties that you will tie to the branches of the tree. The tree acts as a bridge between the divine and human realm manifesting your prayer. I love to watch how the wind will work with me as I tie on yarn I have spun on my spinning wheel with the intention of a healing prayer. The wind will often gather strength as I tie on the prayer, letting me know that my wish is being carried up to the creative forces of the universe.

Burning Sacred Herbs

Burning incense such as sage, juniper, palo santo, or other local herbs can help you carry your intention by asking the wind to take your wishes to the universe. Have ready the sacred herbs you plan on burning. You can use a feather to facilitate your work, as it will help you direct the smoke.

More Tools for Your Toolbox

Communities in shamanic cultures often work with fire to perform a ceremony, and it is seen as an intelligent being. Fire reads our heart and soul desires. Shamans have always worked with fire to get messages. A classic shamanic ceremony is to just sit with a fire or even a candle burning and to hold a question and look at the flame. You may receive your answer as a vision or a feeling in your body, or you may hear a telepathic message.

You might use art supplies that will help you to perform your ceremonial work. If you are working with a group, you can supply these materials for the group, or you can assign everyone different materials to bring.

Some people like to celebrate after a ceremony with eating special foods. Prepare the food before your ceremony so that your celebration becomes a fluid part of your ending.

Consider how to decorate the space you'll be working in, indoors or outdoors. In a room, you might want to include a table with a beautiful scarf or tablecloth over it on which to place the materials and instruments you will use in your ceremony. You might burn some brightly colored candles. Flowers can brighten up a room and help you to feel that a special event is about to occur.

In using an outdoor space, I have seen groups use lanterns, votive candles, or tea candles to light a path to the chosen place of ceremony. Groups might build a beautiful arbor, made with vines or branches and flowers, that everyone passes through to represent leaving their old life behind. As each person walks through the arbor and emerges, they are welcomed into a new time of life and into a holy and sacred space.

You might want to create rock sculptures that bring in a special energy. You may have seen rocks stacked on top of each other along walking trails. These are called cairns. They are often left as markers to help hikers follow a trail, but cairns are also built at ceremonies, oftentimes in the cardinal directions to mark a boundary so that the energy of the ceremony is contained. Or you can simply stack stones or place crystals in a circle, creating a boundary that helps members of the circle know where to stand.

Many people build medicine wheels, putting stones and natural objects in the cardinal directions and performing their ceremony within the medicine wheel. Some even create labyrinths by using rocks to create spiral paths that participants walk through to enter the ceremonial space.

Anointing Materials

In some ceremonies, we welcome each participant by anointing them before they enter the sacred space. The anointing might be done by placing a drop of water or a little daub of earth on a person's third eye or on their crown. I've seen groups use the charcoal left from burning sacred herbs to anoint, as well as flowered or fragrant water. Anointing people as they step into the circle is once again a way of creating a separation between ordinary reality and sacred space. If you intend to use anointing, gather your materials in a bowl before the ceremony.

A Team Is a Powerful Tool

When I lead fire ceremonies, I ask for volunteers to create sacred space, spiritually cleanse the group as they arrive, build the fire beforehand, and safely put out the fire when we are done. I call these volunteers our fire keepers.

If you are working with a group, you can split up tasks of gathering supplies and decorating the space you will be working in. You might all choose to gather wood and make the fire together. Just remember to make sure that after all the preparation everyone is cleansed so that you are ready to officially begin your transformational work.

SETTING UP AN ALTAR CREATES SACRED SPACE

One way to create space is by setting up an altar. The purpose of setting up an altar in a room in your house is to help you move out of an ordinary state of consciousness where you are thinking about your day and move into a state where your psyche knows you're getting ready for special work.

There are many ways to set up an altar. You can set up a very small altar by laying a cloth or rug on the floor of your room, on which you can place a candle, rocks, crystals, flowers, sacred herbs, and so on. Lighting a candle can signal that something special is about to occur. The flame of the candle represents spirit. Burn your favorite incense. You can place the photo of a loved one or spiritual teacher on your altar. Find special objects from nature to add power to your altar.

I live in the high desert in Santa Fe, where we are often in drought. I place a little bowl of water or rose water on my altar to honor the spirit of the land with the gift of water.

Discover for yourself which sacred objects call to you to create sacred space where you perform your spiritual work.

For many people, creating an altar provides a place of comfort to visit any time between your ceremonial work. It is a wonderful place to pray and will bring you tranquility as you sit in silence. After big transformations occur in your life, consider changing your altar to reflect the new phase of life you are stepping into.

You can create an altar outside where you do your ceremonial work. Gather beautiful objects that are meaningful to you and place them on the land. You can build rock cairns or medicine wheels in your special place. This is a wonderful way to bring sacred energy to your land where ceremonial work occurs.

You might live in an apartment or in an urban environment where you cannot keep a permanent altar outside. In this case, you can take home the objects you created your altar with. Or simply create a small altar of stones where others will not notice them. These stones will represent sacred space you can return to when performing your spiritual work.

Many years ago, I was teaching a workshop at a retreat center located in a stunning landscape. I sent my students out to create a personal altar on the land that they could visit every day and prepare before performing healing ceremonies. One of my students not only created an altar by a grand tree near a river running through the property, she also put a note on the ground to say this was her sacred altar. She put a rock over the paper so that it would not blow away.

The next morning, she was walking up to her altar by the tree to perform her preparatory work. Upon arrival, she found a deer urinating on the note that she left stating this was her sacred spot. The universe does have a sense of humor when we are learning how to work in harmony and balance with the rest of life.

Many of us travel with a portable altar to create sacred space in a hotel or a location we visit. Create a simple altar to take with you by using something like a jewelry box and filling it with a bit of sacred herbs, such as sage or cedar, and some small, special objects. You might use beads to create symbolic designs that have special meaning for you to make the box a sacred object. You can pack a small rug, bandana, or handkerchief that you can place your objects on. You might travel with a special photo, rock, crystal, or representation of a helping spirit to place on your altar. You might bring a votive candle to use when it is appropriate.

Use your imagination and feel excitement rising as you envision an altar for your house, office, the land you live on, or a park you perform ceremonies in, and a traveling altar to create sacred space wherever you go.

WORKING WITH EARTH, AIR, WATER, AND FIRE

Once, in an interview about ceremony, the interviewer said, "You said something that I thought was really beautiful and interesting—that the elements that we might be working with and the helping spirits that we've invoked are reading our heart and not necessarily what's going on in our mind. When I heard that, I asked myself, 'What does that mean, for an element like fire to read my heart?'"

I simply loved that question, and I would imagine many of you might be wondering the same thing. I love working with the elements. It's one of my passions to teach people that the elements are incredible allies for us. Earth, air, water, and fire are alive. They are living beings. Just like a tree is alive, fire is alive too.

The elements are intelligent. They are nature, and nature is an intelligent force. I have watched the fire change how it burns when different people come up to the fire during a ceremony to state a prayer. I have watched—with ceremonial work—how the winds change to move a fire in a different direction. We can talk to the elements as allies in partnership, without trying to manipulate them.

Interpreting Omens and Signs

The elements guide us through omens and signs. Years ago, I was teaching a workshop in Santa Fe during a terrible drought. Although we would be performing a fire ceremony at a beautiful fireplace in a meeting room, I still felt uncomfortable. There were trees outside whose branches were hanging too close to the chimney for comfort. Any spark could cause a devastating fire. I asked the land for an omen. I stated to the helping spirits that I was going to cancel the ceremony unless it rained for thirty seconds at 3:00 p.m. At exactly 3:00 p.m., it rained for thirty seconds. This was a great omen to proceed with our fire ceremony. I have continued trusting that the elements will provide omens.

The elements are always presenting signs for us. We have to be more observant of the behavior of nature when we hold a question. We are constantly receiving omens that light our path in life, but we also receive omens at ceremonies. Although there are times when we have to trust our common sense.

At the end of your ceremony, an eagle might fly overhead, symbolizing support from the universe. Or it might start to drizzle on you, which in the practice of shamanism is seen as a blessing. The clouds might clear just when you finish bathing in moonlight. Or a rainbow might appear while you are doing your work. A dragonfly or butterfly might land on your shoulder. Favorite animals might appear at your ceremony, letting you know you are on the right track. A raven might caw at the perfect moment. Claps of thunder might occur at potent times in your ceremonial work, providing an inner knowing that the universe is saying "yes" to your intention. The wind might stir, giving you a sign that your ceremony is complete.

If you are a shamanic journeyer, please understand that your power animal might not necessarily show up as an ally or an omen if it does not live in your locale.

Some omens are very easy to interpret. For example, you take a walk and hold the intention while receiving guidance whether the land you are walking on is the best place for your ceremony. A rainbow appears in the sky, making your answer obvious.

But there are some omens that are not as clear, and it takes time and patience before your inner knowing reveals the meaning to you. Start by asking yourself, "In my wildest imagination, what could this omen mean?" You can journal while holding the intention of your question, and you can journey, if shamanic journeying is part of your practice, or meditate on the answer.

Then there are the omens you might never interpret. I was once guided by my helping spirits to take a walk to ask for an omen to help me resolve a conflict with someone I had a deep connection with. As I walked, a hummingbird appeared and grazed my head. Then a hawk appeared and hit me in the head with its wing. Then they sat together, side by side, on a tree branch. That omen appeared to me in 1999. I still have not figured out the meaning.

Not always being able to interpret a sign is part of the nature of omens. As you continue to work with omens, you will find that many omens are obvious in their meaning, and you get more comfortable with not being able to interpret every sign shown.

Working with omens can be a passive process of observation. It is not an active process where you strain too hard on watching for signs.

One time, I held the intention of asking to be shown how to balance my nervous system. Then one day, a shaman and friend sent me a spontaneous email about the joy she felt after taking a cold plunge. Next, someone out of the blue sent me an email talking about how being in cold water calms the nervous system. If I needed more signs, there was one more to come. I was having dinner with a shamanic teacher who is also a functional nurse practitioner. She told me how she was starting to alternate cold and hot water in her showers to heal her nervous system.

These events occurred within two weeks of each other, and without "straining" to watch for signs, I simply observed how the universe was lighting my path.

In the next chapter, I will talk about how to design a ceremony and about more elements that will facilitate successful and power-filled ceremonies.

3

Preparing for Your Ceremony

Getting into the Right Mind-Set

To begin your ceremonial work, it is important to make sure you step into the unseen realms not burdened by mind chatter. Shamans drum or rattle, dance, and sing for hours to step away from their ordinary life. In our modern world, we don't usually take the time to dance and sing for hours. If you play a shamanic instrument, sing, and dance, you will feel your energy move from your rational mind into your heartspace. It is through the heartspace that we fully partner with helping spirits to make our desired intentions manifest.

This preparation is how shamanic practitioners "power up" for ceremonial work. The word "power" brings up many issues in our culture. We interpret power as being used to dominate and manipulate. In shamanism, powering up is not about control—it is about letting go of control and allowing spiritual energies to work through us. You should feel vital, alive, and filled with spiritual energy during this phase of the work.

I have spoken to many shamanic teachers who have had indigenous people attend their workshops. And they always ask the same question: "Where is the power in your group?" They come to participate in the ceremony and marvel at the stress, trauma, and exhaustion they see in participants' eyes and body language. Many participants look into space, hardly holding their drum or rattle, and simply go through the motions of preparation.

Some people take the opportunity to read their emails during the preparation. Electronic devices should not be allowed in your ceremonies because people will use them. Some people even film ceremonies without permission and post them on YouTube. The solution to this issue is no devices at ceremonies, except ceremonies that people want documented, such as a wedding.

Be a leader and get people moving. Ask them to drum and rattle in a way that brings vitality to the circle, letting their psyche and the spirits know they are ready for the work.

Getting people to sing from the deepest place of their soul gets tricky. Many of us carry a lot of anxiety about singing in public. Yet everything in nature sings. Every living being that is alive sings. If you open your invisible ears, you can hear trees singing.

As a leader, encourage people to sing from their soul—from their inner being and true essence. They might not do it, but if they do, they will be rewarded with feeling power, energy, and joy flowing through their bodies. One of my personal beliefs is that singing and dancing from the soul could be the cure of all depression and anxiety.

I could never hold a tune. But I've taught shamanic songs in every workshop, starting in 1982. At first, we thought the windows would crack when I taught songs. But it was amazing how, over the years, engaging in the joy of singing allowed my voice to open up. Now when I sing invocations, participants remark that it sounds like my voice is coming from some amazing, unearthly realm. It's all about practice.

The same issue applies to some people in our culture about dancing during the preparation phase of a ceremony, but once you get people up and dancing, they typically don't want to stop. It might sound counterintuitive, but leading ceremonies in your community with a smaller group of people makes it easier to get people up drumming, rattling, dancing, and singing. If the intention is strong enough, they can feel the power they must generate. In a large group, a small percentage of people feel that they can hide out, space out, and only engage on a superficial level. But the collective energy is affected when not everyone is fully engaged and participating.

Once people start singing and dancing, they might feel the spiritual energy of a helping and compassionate spirit guiding and empowering their songs and movements.

To prepare for your work, find an activity that moves you away from your job and other daily activities, so you can fully immerse yourself in the invisible realms. Even a symbolic act can be helpful, like washing your face or hands as you imagine releasing negative thoughts.

When performing ceremonies with a group of friends, family members, or members from your community, you can provide simple rattles by putting stones, seeds, or corn in containers that each person can shake. Rattles have been used in shamanic cultures to greet and welcome helping spirits and to help the shaman move into a non-ordinary state of consciousness. When your group gathers, you can shake your rattles and either sing uplifting songs or just let the power of spirit move through you as each person chants whatever sounds emerge from their heart and soul.

For a community that does not embrace the practice of shamanism, have the group sing an uplifting song. This assists people to unburden themselves from their ordinary thoughts and creates an open heart. The power of working with ceremony will be exponential if everyone opens their heart to each other and to the power of spirit. We create an opening in the unseen worlds where our intention is heard, and the power of the universe helps us manifest our desired outcome. Ceremony can help people create a bond that feels like family in the most positive sense of the term.

If you are working alone, take a walk in a park or meditate or perform yoga, tai chi, or qigong to put your daily thoughts aside. Then the doors open into the unseen realms, where manifesting all things is possible.

STEPPING AWAY FROM YOUR ORDINARY LIFE

Shamans in indigenous cultures are known to wear full regalia. This might include wearing a costume or mask of the shaman's helping spirit. Wearing full regalia symbolizes stepping away from ego and personality into connection with the divine.

You do not have to impress or wow the helping spirits or the power of the universe by wearing special clothes when you perform a ceremony. The power of the universe and the helping spirits are not looking at what you are wearing. Wearing special clothes is to help you move into sacred space when you perform ceremonial work. It is a way to plant a seed in your psyche that sacred, holy, and transformational work is taking place.

Ceremony is a magical moment when you can step away from your ordinary life. Make it special. Wear your favorite clothes, a scarf that has important meaning to you, a belt that reminds you that it is time to step into a sacred event, or a piece of jewelry you like to wear for special occasions. Notice what happens when you take time to prepare yourself through washing and dressing for the ceremony. Your mind-set will naturally change as you will feel that something special and sacred is about to happen. Ceremonies are a celebration as we honor our life and those of others present. Think about what you wear to a sacred celebration.

Although alcohol has been used in religious traditions as a sacrament, avoid drinking alcohol before performing a ceremony as it does take away from the ability to stay focused and connected to benevolent spiritual forces during the work. For the same reasons, do not use recreational drugs. While traditional shamans do use plant spirit medicine in performing ceremonies, the use of psychoactive plants is beyond the scope of *The Book of Ceremony*.

Exercise for Letting Go of Your Day

Over time, you will find ways that help you unburden yourself from the thoughts that block you from participating fully in your ceremony. Here is a sample exercise you can try, which gives you an idea of a way of working.

Start by washing your hands and face or brushing your hair. As you do so, focus on what hectic thoughts and beliefs prevent you from being fully present at your ceremony. With the water or using a brush or comb, imagine your interfering state of consciousness is being washed or brushed away. You want your subconscious to be attuned to the power of the work about to take place.

Find an item of clothing that you put on for special events. Look in your mirror and gaze into your eyes. At first when you stare, you see your face just in the surface of your awareness. As you continue to look into your eyes, you will notice your spiritual light shining through. We all have an inner light that shines eternally.

State a decree of your choosing, such as, "I leave my day behind me, and I let go of all thoughts that anchor me into the ordinary realms. I shine my light as I step into sacred space with divine forces that will help me to manifest my intention. I am ready to fully engage in my ceremony now."

Cleansing Ourselves Spiritually Before We Begin

Make sure the land you are working on and all present at a ceremony are spiritually cleansed. You do not want to bring negativity or burdens from your daily life into a transformative ceremony. You do not know who has been on the land before and what they did there, so you want to create a clear and sacred space to begin your work.

Cleansing can be done in many ways. Sacred herbs known for cleansing have been used by traditional cultures, such as sage, cedar, juniper, and sweetgrass in North America; palo santo and copal in South America; and eucalyptus in Australia. What herbs are local to your area that you can burn for cleansing?

You can buy smudge sticks, which are leaves of sage, cedar, or juniper tied in bundles. Sometimes smudge sticks are made by tying a combination of herbs together, such as sage, cedar, juniper, and even lavender. You can also make your own smudge sticks with herbs you have gathered.

Make sure the smudge stick is completely out when ending your ceremony. If you are working with a fire, place what is left of the herbs into the fire. I am known to bring smudge sticks back to my room. Even though they look like they are out, some smudge sticks are still burning inside, and you do not want to leave them anywhere they could start a fire.

Many people burn their cleansing herbs in seashells to honor all the elements—the shell represents water, the herbs are for earth, the smoke represents air, and fire is used to light the herbs.

When working alone, allow the smoke of the herbs to wash over your body and mind. If you are working with a group, one or more of your group members can use a feather to focus the smoke on each participant's body, brushing away any spiritual debris, so all can be fully present at the ceremony.

If people are allergic to burning herbs, then I instruct them to let the volunteers performing the cleansing know and to move quickly through the smoke into the ceremonial space.

Do any cleansing with burning herbs outdoors, so the smoke does not fill the room if people are allergic to fragrances.

There are times when it does not feel correct to burn sacred herbs. It might be too hot and stuffy, or you might be working with people who have a religious objection to being smudged. In these situations, I have people cleanse each other by rattling over them or using the sound of Tibetan bowls, chimes, or bells with the same intention of cleansing each individual present before the ceremony begins. You can use a feather to brush over participants as they release their burdens.

If you are working with a group whose religious beliefs are strong and not shamanically oriented, I have found that singing and welcoming people in with soft bells is a great way to work. Then I make a statement such as this: "We gather together in love and support for each other. I invite each of you to place your hands on your heart and breathe deeply while you step away from your ordinary life, the activities of your day, and the events or thoughts that might keep you anchored to any mind chatter, so you can be fully present to perform this healing or blessing ceremony."

As I encouraged you earlier, you can sing uplifting songs to bring everyone together and create a beautiful, heart-opened sacred space.

Most importantly, you want to make sure that you and others present are stepping into a clean and pristine collective. In this way, the helping spirits can engage with you in a more powerful way, and people present at the ceremony are not being impacted by energetic wounds being carried into the ceremonial space. Keep it pristine!

Greeting and Welcoming Your Helping Allies

The invocation marks the beginning of the ceremony.

In shamanic practice, we use an invocation to welcome and greet the helping allies who are providing invisible help from the unseen worlds during a ceremony. They stand strong with us, sharing their love, light, and protection to make sure our ceremony proceeds in a graceful way. They support the healing, blessing, and celebratory parts of a ceremony.

There is no single correct way to greet these important helping beings who want to assist you in obtaining your desired outcome. However, it's important to make sure that you use the intention to call in "helping and compassionate spirits" or "divine forces," not just "any" spirits.

There are times when a person dies that they do not transcend back to Source. There are a variety of reasons for this that are beyond the scope of this book. There is a wonderful chapter in my book *Awakening to the Spirit World: The Shamanic Path of Direct Revelation* (cowritten with Hank Wesselman) on how shamans work with the dying and death. Some deceased spirits are seen as stuck, and shamans perform healing ceremonies to help them transcend back to Source. These wandering "stuck" spirits are not divine compassionate spirits who can help us with our ceremonial work.

There are many beings from the invisible realms you can honor and invite to support your ceremony. Who you call in depends on your beliefs.

You can add to any invocation greeting the sacred spirits of the mountain, forest, meadow, desert, ocean, river, lake, waterfall, wind, and so on in the location where you are performing your ceremony.

If you are not a shamanic practitioner, call in the presence and support of God, the goddess, guardian angels, or any religious or mystical beings you believe in. Know that they will stand with you as you step forth into performing the ceremony that will transform your life. You can invoke these beings by stating who you are greeting or calling, either out loud or silently.

I use whistling, rattling, and drumming in the greeting process. The beings from the invisible worlds I call in are the spirit of the land I am performing the ceremony on, the helping ancestors of the land, and the power of earth, air, water, and fire. I continue by welcoming and honoring all the nature beings that live on the earth, swim in the water, or fly in the air. I welcome and greet the Hidden Folk, those beings we call the "little people." These races of beings live here in the Middle World with us and caretake the Earth along with us. They are impressed when we show care for ourselves, all of life, and the planet.

I call in the helping spirits—the power animals, guardian spirits, the unseen spiritual teachers, and other allies that I and the group work with in our spiritual practice. I always honor my own ancestors who gave me life and ask participants to honor their ancestors too.

Our Ancestors Are Helping Spirits

It is important when performing ceremonies to call and greet your personal ancestors from both your mother's and father's line. Your ancestors love you and want to see you succeed in life. They want to see you healthy and living a meaningful life.

In my book *Walking in Light*, I share how to journey to your ancestors to learn about the gifts, strengths, and talents they have passed on to you. This is especially important for people who do not know who their ancestors are. So many of our close ancestors immigrated from other countries and integrated into their new culture and left the stories of their lineage behind. Some people were adopted and do not have access to who their ancestors were.

If you have a way to look at old photos of your ancestors or learn more about their personal stories and how they lived, this will help you connect with them. You can place such photos on your altar or even create a separate altar that honors all your ancestors.

In the practice of shamanism, death is perceived as a transition, not an ending. Many cultures believe that when we die, we can evolve to become a helping spirit to support loved ones or other humans.

For many, working with their ancestors can be challenging. We may know about ancestors whose behavior was abusive, or they might have been part of destructive events that do not reflect favorably on them.

But once our ancestors crossed through the veils between the worlds, they became formless beings. They no longer have a personality or ego, for they are now compassionate spirits. Great healing can come from choosing to meet them in a journey or spiritual meditation. This is something for you to decide. We all have the final choice of what ancestors—if any—we wish to meet and honor.

When shamans perform their healing ceremonies on a client or for a community, one of the issues they are looking for is whether there are disharmonious personal connections to close ancestors or throughout the entire ancestral line. If so, they consult with their helping spirits on a ceremony to restore peace.

Shamans today often diagnose our disconnection from our ancestors as a major cause of emotional and physical illness. Many people heal their ancestral disconnection by performing a ceremony to ask for harmony and healing with personal ancestors and throughout a family line. Our ancestors help us navigate through the challenges of life and celebrate our successes.

GREETING OUR SPIRITUAL ANCESTORS

In addition to our familial ancestral line, many of us feel connected to a particular spiritual ancestral lineage. I have known many people who feel strongly drawn to the shamanic traditions of Africa, Australia, Ireland, Egypt, Korea, Central America, Peru, Siberia, and many other places, even though they don't know of any genetic ancestors from those places. They truly feel in their heart, soul, and cells that they are connected to these ancient civilizations.

It is so powerful when we can identify a tradition that feels like "home." This spiritual lineage is as much a part of our ancestry as our biological roots.

If you practice shamanic journeying, you might wish to journey to discover your spiritual roots. These ancient ancestral traditions hold answers, mysteries, tools, and ways for us to work that will help us move to a place of balance and harmony. They can also teach us by sharing their mistakes or the reasons they might have died out, so we can learn not to repeat their errors. If the spirits of another tradition accept and greet you with love and treat you like a family member, they will share fascinating ways of performing ceremonies for healing, for having your wishes and intentions blessed, and for restoring balance in your inner and outer worlds.

Before performing your ceremony, make sure you take the time to prepare through rattling, drumming, singing, dancing, and leaving offerings to welcome your spiritual ancestors. Over time, you will find that they teach you some of the ceremonies they performed, and then as you continue your journeying, you will discover ways to integrate some of the important elements of their work into your own work. Regardless of what they share, having them stand behind you while you perform your shamanic ceremonies is an experience not to be missed!

If you are not drawn to the practice of shamanic journeying, you can do this same discovery work through spending time in nature or meditating on this intention.

Exercise to Greet Your Helping Spirits

Close your eyes and place your hands on your heart. Feel your heart beating and how grateful you are for your life. Or you might feel a wound, a pain, or an issue that brings grief to your heart when you think about the intention of the healing ceremony you are preparing to perform.

As you breathe and focus on the intention of the ceremony, who would you like to call in from the unseen worlds? What helping spirits, ancestors, religious angelic forces, or mystical figures bring comfort to your soul when you think of asking invisible allies to support the work ahead?

Take your time and simply reflect on this question. You might sit and drum or rattle during your time of reflection. Or take a walk in nature. Listen to spiritual music and reflect on the invisible beings you wish to invite to your ceremony as ones who will support you.

When you begin your ceremony, greet these beings out loud. Again, you can drum, rattle, or use another instrument such as a flute, a guitar, Tibetan bowls, bells, chimes, or any instrument that brings you into sacred space. Remember the invocation is all about creating sacred and holy space.

In some shamanic cultures, petition is used to call in the helping spirits. An example of a petition is "Please help me manifest the intention of my healing ceremony."

Some shamans and community members use the power of decree. Instead of asking for help, state an invocation that strongly acknowledges that the help of the spirits is already here. Here's an example of a decree: "Thank you for joining this ceremony and adding your power and strength to manifest my intention in a graceful way."

GREETING THE CARDINAL DIRECTIONS

Greeting the cardinal directions is a common practice in shamanic cultures. There is no one right way shamans greet the directions. Honoring the directions was often based on weather patterns in the local area, specifically which direction the wind entered the land.

You must find your own way to greet the directions. We all know East is the direction of the rising sun, and West is the direction of the setting sun. The direction away from the equator reminds us of winter and cold, while the opposite direction invokes a feeling of warmth.

As I shared in "Gathering Your Materials" in chapter 2, some people make medicine wheels that they stand within when doing ceremonial work. You might find objects in nature, such as a feather, rock, or crystal. Or you might light a candle or put out a bowl of water to honor qualities you feel represent a given direction.

Exercise to Call in the Directions

As you did when calling in helping spirits, take some time to reflect on the directions.

Stand and face East. Close your eyes and place your hands on your heart. As you focus your imagination on the East and the rising sun, what feelings emerge for you?

Turn South and let your imagination soak in the qualities that come to you associated with the South.

Face West and take a deep breath and exhale. In your mind's eye, see and feel the sun setting. What associations does this bring to you?

Next, face North and observe how you feel in your heart. What meaning does the North hold for you?

In some cultures, the direction of Below is greeted to honor Earth. And the direction of Above is welcomed to honor Sky. Lastly, the direction of Within is acknowledged to honor the power of spirit and divine light that resides in each us.

FOLLOW YOUR HEART

In shamanism, there is no right way or consensus on how to perform your invocations. Every culture works in their own way, which has been passed down by their ancestors.

Many of us in the Western world were not taught about the power of the unseen worlds. We must "invent" new and fresh ways to work that speak to our heart and soul. Then we make our work relevant to our needs and avoid copying ceremonies performed by cultures who have not given us permission to work in their way. Their ceremonies were created for their community's specific needs.

How do you wish to work? Take time to reflect on this in silence. This is not a rational process, for the helping spirits of the unseen worlds care about our heart's desires. As long as you follow what your heart calls you to do, your invocation will be successful.

Work with your helping spirits in cooperation and collaboration. Never try to manipulate them. Be honorable and respectful toward the compassionate ancestors of the land. When you do, miracles do occur in your ceremonial work.

Prepare the instruments you wish to use to greet the helping spirits. I begin by whistling, which is how many shamans call in their helping spirits.

I call in the power of love and light. In this way, I am surrounded by only the highest beings as I work, and I do so for any group I am working with. In working with a group, I state out loud: "This is a circle of strength. This is a circle of power. We have gathered together in love and light to support each other as we do our important work to heal ourselves, all in the web of life, and for the Earth. We join our hearts together in love. And only that which is of the light is welcomed into our circle."

Once you have completed saying your invocation, you want to add these words: "The work begins now." In this way, you mark to the community present and to the helping spirits that the preparation has been completed, and the structure and next phase of the ceremony will now be performed.

CREATING A SUCCESSFUL CEREMONY

There are key elements that will help you create a successful ceremony. It is so important to keep your concentration and focus while performing your sacred work. Imagine trying to create a positive outcome while your mind is wandering to what you have to do when you are finished. There is no focused energy to fuel your work.

Using your imagination is also important for positive results. You need to imagine that your wish is fulfilled. Opening your heart creates a powerful channel for the spiritual forces to join you in partnership during your ceremony.

Whether you perform your ceremony alone or with a group, keep the ceremony simple and reflect on the timing. In shamanic cultures, ceremonies often begin at sunset and end at sunrise. With the fast pace of modern life, if you make the ceremony too complex, your mind will wander. People today are not accustomed to holding their focus for a long time. If your ceremony goes on for too long, people will become distracted and bored, taking away from the power of the ceremony. This is something to reflect on as you design your ceremonies.

It is a wonderful experience to perform a ceremony with a group of friends. It will bring you so much closer. In doing this, it is important that everyone has a task, such as helping to spiritually cleanse the group, preparing the space you are working in by cleansing it and calling in the helping spirits, bringing offerings to create sacred space, and gathering materials. You might include a ceremonial fire, in which case you can all build the fire together.

You can greet and thank the helping spirits for their assistance in creating your desired outcome. Or if you do not work with helping spirits, you can all state your prayers and wishes together to the creative forces of the universe, God, the goddess—whoever you work with in your spiritual life.

One brilliant shamanic teacher had volunteer fire keepers pray during her two-week summit where she had other authors presenting lectures and experiential practices to navigate challenging times. What a beautiful way to keep the ceremony held in love, whether your ceremony is a one-time event or continues over weeks or months.

4

Performing
Your Ceremony

You will discover that there are a variety of ways to design a ceremony. You might begin by designing your own personal ceremonies. In time, you might feel comfortable sharing and inviting friends and loved ones to perform ceremonies with you using the exponential power of a group. One day, your passion may arise to bring your ceremonial work into your community to provide healing and to ask for blessings of harmony to enrich the lives of everyone—in your community and in the world.

Setting Your Intention

Intention creates action. It is important for you to get clear on what you are asking for when you perform a ceremony. In life, we set intentions in conscious and unconscious ways. If you take time to reflect on major changes in your life, you might notice that you were thinking about making a change.

In truth, life is a ceremony. As you work with performing ceremonies, you will notice how your everyday wishes and intentions begin to manifest on some level—in ways that might surprise you. You might be daydreaming about healing an issue in your life. Then the right people show up in your life to help light your path and show you the steps you need for healing. You might be considering a trip you wish to take, and you find all the pieces falling into place in an unexpected way to make the trip happen. We can often track how our life has unfolded by reflecting on our past intentions.

The more conscious you are of the intentions you set, the more you will notice how intention does create action and helps to manifest your goals in the present and future. Developing a disciplined practice around setting intentions allows you to work in partnership with helping spirits, God, the goddess, and the creative forces of the universe to manifest your dreams.

Take some time before you perform a ceremony to reflect on what you are truly asking for. If you have a practice of shamanic journeying, discuss your intention with your helping spirits. They will guide you in creating the correct wording so that you ask for something you want to see manifest. I personally journey and discuss the intention I wish to state with my main power animal. He helps me shape the language of my intentions. He will show me the vibration that will be created with my words. He asks me to stop and reflect on each word. I imagine if each word will be a blessing for my desired outcome.

Whether through journeying, meditation, prayer, or contemplation, take some time for reflection in silence. A good practice is to walk or sit in nature. Drop into a quiet place and perform the practice of deep listening. Gaze into a body of water or out over the landscape, sit and watch the flames of a fire, or listen to messages from the wind. This will move you into a shamanic and meditative state of consciousness where you will receive a message or feel an intuitive knowing of the right intention to set.

If you have another divination practice besides shamanic journeying, you can turn to your divination tools to set an intention. I often pick a tarot card that represents something I need to release during a ceremony or a positive quality I need to call into my life. Some people work with a pendulum to set their intention.

Shamans learn to use multiple divination tools in their own practice. You will find your own divination tools over time. One of my favorite tools is simply drinking a cup of tea in the morning when my mind is quiet and my inner spiritual knowing emerges effortlessly.

I advise against stating open-ended intentions. For example, you could get surprising results when setting an intention such as "Bring me the lessons I need to learn." You might end up experiencing tragedy or learning the invaluable lessons that come from pain or illness.

Give a little bit more information about what you are asking of the helping spirits and the universe. In the example above, instead of asking for any situation that provides a growth experience, you might ask for gentle and supportive people entering your life to teach you about the power of love, for a joyful relationship to manifest, or for a wonderful job that fills your life with meaning. As you continue your ceremonial work, you will find yourself becoming courageous and stating your intention in stronger ways with your authentic desires.

As always, your heart will lead you to the right intention for any ceremony you perform.

Some people use a journal to write down their ceremonial intentions and track results of each ceremony they perform. This can serve as a road map for following where your spiritual path is taking you. On the negative side, it can get you too focused on watching and waiting for results.

Part of our evolution with working with shamanic ceremonies is to stay present, do the work, and let go of the outcome—not easy for us humans who want to witness immediate results in just the way we want to see them. It is important to recognize that shamanism works on a spiritual level that is a timeless dimension. The helping spirits can see a bigger picture than we can see through the eyes of ego. The true challenge, and also the gift, is for us to learn how to express what we desire and then let go of when and how our desire manifests.

Our ego does not always know how to judge if a ceremony was a success or failure, for the ego creates a mental expectation of what should happen. In truth, the helping spirits and the power of the universe hold a different picture then we can see with our ordinary eyes. Ceremonies performed from a place of love, honor, and respect are successful—perhaps not always in the way our ego imagined, but manifesting what our soul, our essence, our inner wisdom is asking for. In our modern-day culture, we tend to try to control the natural changes that life brings. As we "loosen our grip," we effortlessly bring more grace to us as we enter into the organic flow of life.

The helping spirits and the divine forces of the universe are part of our team. They often create outcomes that will bring us gifts we had not imagined when we need them most, which might not be the timing our ego hoped for. In our culture, we often focus too much on wanting to witness an immediate "win." Consider a delicious meal being cooked slowly or planting seeds and taking the time to nurture them and watch them grow. The result of our ceremony is an organic process.

On the other hand, I have seen ceremonies that immediately resulted in exactly what a person asked for. This is not because they were somehow "worthy" of a miraculous result—it is simply a sign that the ceremony was performed at the right time.

It is all part of the great mystery. We all need to learn how to surrender and find peace with it.

When you use shamanic journeying or other divination tools, or practice deep listening in nature, you flow into a sacred space where you have access to what your heart and soul are calling for instead of only relying on what your ego wants. Often our ego is asking for something that is *not* in our best interest. To manifest the desire and passion of our soul is always going to bring in the goodness of life or help us release a pain or wound that prevents us from living a healthy life filled with joy and peace. Of course, life brings us challenges to grow, stretch, and evolve. As we live here on Earth, everything that is alive is given continual challenges to help it grow.

You can always perform a ceremony to ask that the circumstances given for growth are modified so that you can ride the waves a bit easier. For example, if life has brought you to a place where everything is dissolving before your eyes—you are having problems at work, you have to move, your relationship is falling apart—you can ask for resolution in a ceremony. You still honor the messages that are calling you to change and create a healthier life, but you might ask that the messages come in less dramatic ways.

It is important to recognize that the outcome of your ceremony is not in your control. As humans, we often have to walk through the fire to evolve into a more balanced and healthier state of life. Practicing ceremony does not exempt you from life's storms, but it does give you a powerful tool for riding them out.

COMMON QUESTIONS THAT ARISE WHEN SETTING AN INTENTION

When we first begin designing our ceremony, our intention and excitement build within. Sometimes, our rational mind gets in the way of that initial excitement. We begin to doubt whether our intention is correct or worry whether the ceremony will be successful.

How can you know if your ordinary thinking mind is setting your intention or if your intention is arising from your expansive heartspace to serve your highest good? People often ask me how I know if it is my "small self" or "higher Self" setting the intention.

I truly believe that we have to start somewhere. If we start with an intention, we open the door into the invisible realms, where change happens. Even if the intention does not reflect what your soul is calling for, the universe recognizes your desire for healing, blessing, and change. This leads to successful ceremonies. Over time, you will learn how to access deeper places within your inner world where your intentions will reflect the depth of your soul. Do not be afraid to begin your ceremonial work. Allow the work to evolve over time.

For example, I lead a lot of fire ceremonies to release beliefs that prevent people from using their full creativity. Many students are concerned that their real blockages are in the subconscious—if they don't know what the belief is, how can they ask to release it? My advice is that it is okay to start by releasing a belief you are consciously aware of. The ceremony will at least open the door for healing to begin.

I believe the helping spirits, God, the goddess, the creative force of the universe, and the elements (earth, air, water, fire) we work with while performing our ceremonies know what we are asking for on a spiritual level, even if our conscious mind does not.

Part of the work is to keep asking, "What is my personal desire and what is coming from my soul's desire?" Your soul, or your higher Self, holds the knowledge and wisdom of what needs to be manifested for your highest good. It takes time and commitment to explore the passion of your soul.

The exploration has to start somewhere. Over time, as we get experience in performing ceremonies, we gain a greater ability to tell the difference between what our ego wants and what the bigger picture is. There is a bigger picture going on in the collective right now too. We need to have an intention, hold to our vision, keep our concentration and focus while performing any ceremony, and simultaneously let go of the outcome.

As you can imagine, this gets tricky. No one wants to be disappointed by the results of their ceremonial work. There is a paradox we all dance. From a human perspective, we don't know the bigger picture. But it is also your destiny to participate in the game of life fully and to add your creative and heart energy to ask for a positive change in your own life and in the world.

It is challenging to surrender our preconceptions about the outcome and timing of a ceremony. The universe helps to create change with the right timing, and that might not be the timing you expected. This is where trust comes in. And trust comes from experience. You will gain more trust in the intelligence of the universe as you perform ceremonies over time.

Are You an Observer or Engaged in Your Ceremony?

One day I was sitting with my husband in our living room. We have big windows where we can look out onto the hills, trees, and the wealth of birds that come to drink water and eat. As I was sitting and watching the beauty of nature, I realized that I was observing the scene as if I were watching TV, as if everything I was watching outside was two-dimensional.

When I go outside and fully interact with the land and engage all my senses, I am stepping into a full three-dimensional experience. When I watch the birds, I am part of the landscape that they are in. Stepping in fully with all my senses open and alive gives me an entirely different experience than sitting on the couch watching nature as an observer.

In the same way, when we perform ceremonies as a virtual journey or meditation, we often find ourselves watching the ceremony instead of engaging.

There are times when we cannot go out and physically perform a ceremony. And there are times when we work with a group of practitioners who are joining together from all over the world. In these times, working with virtual ceremonies is a great choice for ceremonial work. Even with performing a virtual ceremony, you can engage all your senses to fully see, hear, feel, smell, and taste your experience in the unseen worlds.

Instead of observing your virtual ceremony like a movie, use your imagination to create the scenes you gaze upon, the fragrances you smell, textures that you touch with your fingers, foods you eat, and sounds that you hear. You want to experience yourself fully engaging in your ceremony as if you were actually performing it in the ordinary realm.

For example, when performing a virtual fire ceremony, see and smell the smoke and hear the fire crackling. Fully open your senses to feel the texture of the earth you are standing on and smell the fragrances in the air. Gaze at the beauty of the sky and feel the rays of the sun filling you with energy or feel the awe of looking up into the night sky.

When performing a virtual ceremony at the sea, smell the salt in the air, listen to the waves, touch the water, feel the wind on your face and the coolness on your skin.

The key to participating in a powerful virtual ceremony is making sure you have stepped fully into the unseen worlds and the landscape where the ceremony is taking place.

CLOSING YOUR CEREMONY

Once your ceremony is complete, consider leaving an offering of thanks. I give cedar to the fire in thanks and give offerings to the land

and the helping spirits. As I shared earlier, you can leave a variety of drinks, food, and herbal offerings that are safe for the environment. Be certain to clean up everything that is not an offering to honor the area where your ceremony took place.

Grounding

You might not realize it at the time of your ceremony, but your state of mind changes. You might feel a state of bliss and joy in doing such sacred work. It is so important to ground after performing a ceremony. You don't want to end feeling spaced out and losing your balance as you walk away or being inattentive when you drive. You want to feel completely rooted into yourself and to the earth after your ceremony.

I imagine myself connected to a tree and experience my deep roots going down into the earth. If I am in a place in nature, I might sit with a tree for a while, or even sit and feel my connection to my body and the earth.

Some people crash land after a ceremony. They do not engage in an appropriate closing to ground themselves. Then the next day, they might feel ill or spaced out. The key is to always ground to end your ceremony in a graceful fashion.

Exercise for Grounding

Your ceremony is over—congratulate yourself and your group on a job well done. This is a good beginning way to ground, for you are saying to yourself and your unconscious that your work is done for now.

Stand and raise your arms up to the sky. Feel your feet planted on the earth. Next, shake your hands and arms to discharge any spiritual energy that might need to be released. Let the loving spiritual energies flow through you, down your body, through your feet, and into the earth. Place your hands on the earth and let light-filled spiritual energies flow.

Next, imagine deep roots growing from your feet into the earth, like the roots of a tree. Feel the solidity of your body. Bring into your heart energies those who you care about and bring you joy. Even if your ceremony leaves you in tears, remember what and whom you love.

Place your hands on your heart, feeling your heartbeat. Recognize how much you love yourself even if you have to fake it. We are not that good at loving ourselves in our culture. If your eyes are closed, open them, and you should feel grounded.

Another tip for grounding is to eat a healthy meal. Or lean against a tree that helps you root back into your body like it roots into the earth. You can do this either as a meditation experiencing yourself sitting with a tree or by going out into nature. Holding a rock while focusing on your connection to your body is also very grounding. Some people have their favorite grounding crystals or stones that they hold.

Whether you do your grounding exercise outside or through a journey or meditation does not matter. You just want to make sure you feel completely in your body. You will still have a spiritual glow—I hope you do. But let that glow shine through you as you bridge Heaven and Earth, with your heart and grounded presence on this Earth.

These techniques are just suggestions—experiment and learn what works best for you!

WHEN THINGS SEEM TO GO WRONG

You might be at a ceremony where a person's cell phone goes off, a stranger shows up during your work, or somebody in your circle gets ill. Everything that happens in a ceremony is part of the divine play of the ceremony. Sometimes things happen that make us laugh or cry. The key is to hold your center and to get a person comfortable if they need help. You can gently remove any disrupting factor from the ceremonial space—but continue the ceremony. Everything that happens is part of that magic moment. The group will follow your lead if you remain calm, keep your cool, and continue to stay centered.

Sometimes during or after a ceremony, a participant might experience nausea. From a shamanic point of view, nausea is stuck power that is not flowing. This stuck energy is easy to release by dancing, singing, or putting your hands on the earth to get the energy moving.

In the early 1990s, I taught a Soul Retrieval Training in Tennessee. The training took place during Hurricane Opal. The last night of the workshop, the group performed a fire ceremony to release old wounds that no longer served them as they moved forward in their healing practice. Each person made an effigy to release into the fire.

The rain and wind were so strong from the hurricane that we could not work outside. There was a tiny fireplace in a small room that we could use, but we would all have to stand like sardines to fit in the room. I knew I could make it work as we created sacred space. You can create sacred space anywhere. The room does not have to be perfect.

We started to build our fire when someone ran into the room and exclaimed that it had stopped raining. I yelled to the group, "Everyone take a piece of wood, and let's run to the meadow to the large fire pit."

We ran with our wood and talismans. I called in the helping spirits, thanked the weather spirits for their cooperation, and we built a sacred fire. We drummed, rattled, sang, and danced as each person did their work to release their wound, their burden, into the fire.

When the last person released their burden into the fire, I quickly closed the ceremony by thanking the helping spirits, the ancestral spirits of the land, the weather spirits, and the support from our circle, cheering on each person as they did their personal healing work. And I declared, "Our work is done for now."

During my closing words, the hurricane returned in full force, and we ran back to our lodge, drenched but laughing, and so grateful for the cooperation of helping spirits.

We were not so lucky at another Five-Day Soul Retrieval Training I taught in New Mexico. The day of our fire ceremony, we got such heavy monsoon rains that we did not believe we could build a fire that night. But we had dedicated volunteer fire keepers who said they would try. To our amazement, they were successful.

We put on our rain ponchos and ceremoniously walked to our sacred fire. We used our rattles so that our drums would not get destroyed by the rain, and we danced and sang and called in the helping spirits. We thanked the rain for blessing our work. We completed our ceremony and went to bed.

The next morning, we talked about what a magical experience it had been to have everyone in ponchos, for we could not see anyone's face. We did not know who was working in turn with the fire. We all felt that we were in a sea of oneness and that the anonymity of each person added to the magic of the ceremony. We were not individuals working on our own wounds but were part of a collective working on different aspects of the wounds we all carry as humans. The work each of us did impacted our own personal healing.

I could write volumes on the amazing experiences I have witnessed over years of leading ceremonies. We once had to use a sewer grate on a road to build our fire, and once, due to fire danger, we could only place an inch of our effigies into a fire—we buried the rest on the land. These two ceremonies were among the most powerful I have attended, as we had to use our creativity to be flexible with what arose.

What I learned over time is that there are no mistakes. If you go with the flow and make adaptations to your ceremonies, you will see that all that occurred was simply perfect and meant to be. It is important to be flexible and change the structure of your ceremony if you need to.

Once you call in the helping spirits or state your intention, trust that your ceremony will unfold in a perfect way. Sometimes what occurs will make you laugh. In shamanic cultures, the community does not talk about a ceremony in a judgmental way or compare it to other ceremonies. The only response at the end of a ceremony is how beautiful it was.

How Many Times Does a Ceremony Need to Be Repeated?

There are some ceremonies that only have to be done once. If you are honoring a phase of the moon or season, you only need to perform your ceremony until the next time you feel called to honor a shift in cycles. If you are blessing a newborn baby or a new house, performing one ceremony is perfect. These are just some examples.

If you are releasing a burden or wound you have been carrying for years, you might need to repeat your ceremony over time until you feel the healing has taken place. You will find that as you continue to perform releasing ceremonies, layers of old hurts might emerge to be healed. In this way, you keep working to release the core issues that prevent you from living the life you desire and using your full creative potential.

For example, you might perform a blessing ceremony of bringing to you the goodness of life. After the ceremony, you feel like you do not deserve the goodness of life. This feeling is a signal to help you explore what needs to be released so that you can accept love and blessings from others and the universe.

In shamanic cultures some ceremonies are completed in minutes, weeks, or months as they need to be built upon or repeated.

You will know when a ceremony is done and when you need to work with another layer. Let your intuition guide you.

Designing a Successful Ceremony

Here is a summary of elements to incorporate in designing a ceremony. This summary includes bringing friends and loved ones and your community into the work.

1. **Keep It Short**   The most powerful ceremonies are those where you open the door to the invisible realms and state your intention and keep the ceremony to the point. A key to a successful ceremony is concentration and focus. If you create a long and complex ceremony, participants tend

to lose interest, lose focus, and start to drift away. The ceremony then loses power.

2. **Prepare**   Do your preparation work. Make sure you call in your helping and compassionate spirits as well as the helping ancestral compassionate spirits of the land. Give thanks to the helping spirits to guide you in your words as you speak and lead a powerful and healing ceremony.

3. **Set a Clear Intention**   Be clear on the intention of the ceremony. In performing a ceremony, your intention is heard by the helping spirits and the power of the universe. These helping spiritual forces work in partnership with you to manifest your desire. Consult with your helping spirits to make sure your wording reflects the intention that is for the highest good.

4. **Create an Altar**   As mentioned, you can create an altar at home or in nature. You can even just bring flowers. You can invite people to bring or leave objects on the altar. Remind them to take their precious objects home at the end unless they are consciously left as a gift for the land. You can choose to work with elaborate decorations to create sacred space or simply just speak from your heart.

5. **Greet Participants**   When working in a group, welcome each participant personally into the circle. This will help you to relax and make people feel welcomed as they step into doing something that might feel unknown or a little scary to them. The simple act of greeting each person with a smile dissolves suspicions.

6. **Be Confident in Your Opening Words**   When leading a group ceremony, prepare your opening sentence. Once you state your opening sentence, you will find your inner

spirit speaking through you. Put on an air of confidence even if you are nervous. If you do not seem confident, a group you are leading will not feel safe and will not fully participate in the ceremony. They will observe without fully participating.

7. **The Opening Invocation**   Lead an opening invocation to get people to move their energy from their thinking mind into their heart and to welcome each person into the circle. Ask people to take some deep breaths while placing their hands on their heart and welcoming each person into the circle while wishing for the best outcome for everyone who has joined the ceremony. Your opening invocation needs to end with letting everyone know that the work is beginning now.

8. **Release Your Burdening Thoughts**   Invite people to leave their ordinary thoughts and concerns behind and to fully join in and not just observe. You can get people into the right place by leading inspirational songs or playing musical instruments to open their heart. In some ceremonies, I set out a big bowl or drum and invite people to place something that represents an anchor to their ordinary world that needs to be released before stepping into ceremonial space. This might be a piece of jewelry, a watch, a cell phone, or a paper with a burden written on it. Participants take back their possessions once the ceremony has been closed.

9. **Give Clear Instructions**   Explain the steps of the ceremony you will be leading. In this way, people know what to expect, and this helps them maintain a focus.

10. **Invite People to Pray**   Before closing the ceremony, open a space for people to share prayers, asking that the goodness

of the ceremony may radiate to others and the world. This is also a time to thank everyone who participated and helped create the ceremony.

11. **Inspire Your Community**   Close by thanking the helping spirits and saying inspiring words to your community. Your helping spirits will give you healing words to end with, just listen to their guidance as you speak. Make sure everyone in the community is grounded.

12. **Sharing Messages**   Leave some space for participants to share messages that came through the helping spirits during the ceremony or to share omens that might have been seen during a ceremony. A compassionate spirit might share a message with a participant such as "learn to love yourself," "trust," "we love you," "you are protected," "remember to shine your light," "don't lose hope," "miracles are possible," "trust your intuition," "focus on the beauty of life," "honor and respect all of life," "let your tears flow," and so on. People might also wish to share feelings that came up during the ceremony.

13. **Celebrate**   If you are working with a group, you can serve refreshments after the ceremony, so people can meet each other and talk about the work. This is a perfect time for adding a grounding practice.

The magic of ceremony is being able to leave your ordinary life behind and step into a sacred space. In this space, you can truly participate with others who are opening their hearts along with you to create positive change and help the stated intention manifest.

Make sure that your intention for your ceremonies carries the energy of love, honor, and respect. Please do not perform any ceremonies out of wanting vengeance or to curse someone. This is not what the evolution of shamanism is about. Performing ceremonies should only be used for healing and to share love, light, support, honor, and respect.

In the chapters ahead, you will read about different ceremonies. As you read the upcoming chapters, you will get ideas of how to structure the middle of your ceremony. Over time, you will start to see that the most powerful ceremonies that you perform are the ones you have improvised and made your own.

5

Additional Guidelines for Your Ceremonial Work

The Initiatory Aspect of Ceremonies

We have to let a part of ourselves be willing to die if we are going to emerge from ceremonies renewed and reborn. Ceremonies can also awaken a natural detoxification process, releasing impurities from our body, emotions, and spirit.

There is the big death you go through at the end of your life, but throughout life, there are little deaths that happen whenever something is taken from you—whether you lose a job, become ill, break up with a partner, or lose your home in a catastrophic event. These losses are a form of initiation—a part of you lets go, and something new is born.

Any change we experience in life is an initiation.

Whenever we perform a ceremony—whether it is a small one or a big one—we come out feeling different, but in a good way. Even if we can't verbalize what feels different, our ego starts to be sculpted away, allowing our spiritual light to shine through. Divine forces partner with our inner divine to reshape, reform, and resculpt our life and our lifestyle, bringing us to a deeper spiritual place where our spirit can carry us through and provide solutions to challenges that seem impossible to work with and heal. We feel filled with spiritual energies and connected to our authentic identity as we shed qualities others projected onto us.

Sometimes these initiatory experiences can awaken our invisible senses. A practitioner might become clairvoyant, opening their invisible eyes that see visions in the unseen realms. Or a practitioner might awaken their invisible ears and become clairaudient, getting verbal messages from the helping spirits. A practitioner might tap into the power of clairsentience, where they feel the information on a body level of awareness—we often refer to this as "feeling it in our bones."

Whatever occurs, we must learn how to surrender and accept what life brings for us. This is what initiation is about. When you are in the middle of a firewalk, you cannot think about whether you want to complete your firewalk while you're actually walking on red-hot coals. You will get burned. It is your inner spirit that carries you through an initiation such as a firewalk and all the challenging initiations we experience in life.

We have to let go of expectations when experiencing an initiation brought on by any ceremony. There is a process where we just have to let spirit carry us through. That's not always easy, especially when we do not rationally understand the big picture.

Surrender and acceptance are two important aspects of being able to fully participate in the changes of life, initiation, dismemberment, and rememberment, leaving us feeling renewed and refreshed, with our spiritual light shining through. We go through a process of dissolution that leads to illumination.

Whether or not you experience your desired outcome after performing a ceremony, it is still important to state your intention, do your preparation work, create sacred space, and perform your ceremonial work.

With ceremony, you take the opportunity to ask for healing to happen and for a particular intention to manifest—and then you also have to accept that there is a bigger picture that you might not be aware of.

I can tell you that after performing ceremonies alone and with groups for more than thirty-five years, wonderful manifestations of healing, blessing, and change do happen.

Performing ceremonies can become habit-forming in the most positive sense.

The Difference Between Willpower and Strength of Spirit

When we face a difficult situation, we tend to rely on our willpower and our thinking mind to help us step up to the challenge. But in reality, it is the strength of our inner spirit that carries us through initiations.

Many years ago, one of my helping spirits shared with me that using willpower does not show strength. Real strength is when one can surrender to the powers that be.

In our modern culture, we focus on using our willpower and improving our rational mind. In shamanic cultures, spiritual strength—meaning living a shamanic way of life—is what helps the people survive. Community members learn to transform their negative thinking, let the goodness of life unfold, be compassionate, honor their interconnectedness, respect the web of life, and live in harmony with nature.

They understand that what we see in the outside world is a reflection of our inner landscape. They do their inner gardening work to develop a sense of beauty, and they nurture their spiritual light so that it shines into the world and is reflected back to them.

In shamanic cultures, the power of will and spirit intertwine. In our culture, "powering through" with our will is our typical behavior. Powering through a ceremony will not lead to success. Only by standing in our spiritual strength will our ceremony provide us with our desired results.

While I was writing *The Book of Ceremony*, my spiritual teacher Isis and other compassionate spirits shared with me that the entire planet is going through an initiation. We all need to be resculpted so that we can live on this Earth in a healthier way and learn about the power of love, light, honor, and respect. My helping spirits shared that the most important way to thrive through the coming times is by strengthening our spirit.

Living a healthy life means integrating practices that nurture and strengthen all aspects of body, mind, and spirit. In the Western world, we focus on strengthening our body and mind. We allow ourselves to become distracted by nurturing our rational mind through collecting more intellectual material. And many of us focus on building strong muscles through exercise.

By adding spiritual practices and performing ceremonial work, we learn to surrender to the natural flow and process of death and rebirth. These are not separate processes—they are a flow. Life is a flow.

The initiation we are going through is a classic shamanic initiation in which we can't "think" our way through or physically "power through" with our muscles.

Initiations can be perilous. When you can't think your way out, and physical strength does not help, an initiation wears you down to a place where your mind gives up in complete despair with no road map out of the challenge you are facing. Your body gives in also, as you are too worn down to continue. Then your inner spiritual fire awakens, and you surrender to the true strength of inner spiritual power that knows no obstacles, pain, or suffering on any level.

I do not publicly broadcast the initiations I have been through. I've written about my near-death experiences, but frankly, they pale in comparison to the lifelong initiations I have been through, when I felt as if I had been dropped blindfolded out of an airplane with no road map to help me walk through the foreign terrain. So far in my sixty-five years of initiations, my inner spirit has carried me even when it looked like I could not muster enough strength to make it through.

I am writing about initiations from my knowledge of shamanism but also from my own life experience. In today's world, the divine forces are asking us to awaken our inner spirit, to develop the spiritual muscles needed to swim through the deep, dark waters until we eventually emerge into pure luminescence, in touch with our authentic spiritual identity and light.

Virtual Ceremonies

There is certainly a great power in performing ceremonies in a sacred room in your house or in nature. You design the ceremony, gather the necessary materials, and work with the elements. And when working with a group, everyone can talk together, hold hands, dance and sing, bond in a deep way, and celebrate at the end of the ceremony.

At the same time, we live in an age where technology can assist us in gathering people from around the world to perform ceremonies for personal healing, blessings, and healing the Earth. I have had the opportunity through teleconferencing courses and webinars to lead virtual ceremonies in which hundreds or thousands of people from around the world are working together in support of each other, all of life, and the Earth.

Imagine the exponential energy that is created in working in this way. These virtual ceremonies are usually recorded, so people who could not participate during the live ceremony can perform the ceremony later. In shamanism, we work outside of time, so it does not matter when people join in on a virtual ceremony—the power just keeps building as people do the work over time.

In today's world, peers, friends, and family might live in different states or countries. A wonderful exercise is to create a ceremony that establishes a sacred altar in the unseen realms where people can meet, pray, and perform ceremonial work together. Such an altar can also serve the needs of a group that meets on a regular basis by giving them a place to connect and perform ceremonies in the unseen world when meeting physically isn't possible.

You might find that there are friends and family who do not live near you but want to join together to create a ceremony for healing or blessings. Working virtually is a powerful way of joining together no matter where everyone lives.

SETTING UP AN ALTAR IN NONORDINARY REALITY

Here is an example of a shamanic meditation to create an altar in the nonordinary realms.

Start with your preparation work to step away from your daily concerns and call in your unseen allies to support your ceremony. Again, you can call in God, the goddess, or any divine being you work with.

When performing ceremonies with people living in different locales or who might choose to work virtually, set up a virtual sacred place where you can all meet and work together. This altar is a place where you are going to return from time to time. It is a place where you can go between spiritual meetings with your group or to perform your ceremony there. You can visit this space to pray and to receive comfort.

While journeying or meditating, use your imagination to place special objects that can empower your circle, and place prayers for yourself, others, and the planet. This altar remains spiritually cleansed by helping guardian spirits.

The meditation I will now share is an example of how to set up an altar in the invisible realms. Always feel the freedom to adapt this meditation to include landscapes you wish to walk in and objects that you wish to place on your altar in the unseen realms. This example will guide you to a sacred space in a meadow. You might want to create your altar by a river or ocean. Your decision will be based on where you live as well as the spiritual guidance you receive. In my trainings, I lead people to a sacred room in nonordinary reality, and we call it our altar room.

Guided Meditation to Create
an Altar in the Unseen Realms

Listen to drumming or other shamanic music. Or play your favorite meditation or spiritually expansive music. Set an intention that you want to lift the veils between the seen and unseen realms. Your starting place will be the room you are journeying or meditating in.

Take some deep breaths. Close your eyes and breathe deeply as you move into a peaceful and centered place. Imagine walking up to the door of your apartment or house; then open your door and step through a veil onto a path in nature.

Walk down the path, opening your senses. Observe the beauty of nature. You might be surrounded by trees or other greenery. Gaze at the sky. Feel your feet connecting with the earth as you walk on the path. Feel the texture of the earth. Listen with awe and wonder to the surrounding sounds of nature. Take a deep breath and smell the fragrances of the earth, the plants, and the trees as you walk this path of exquisite beauty. Feel the gentle breeze caressing your face. Observe the rocks, birds, insects, animals, flowers, and other beings of nature. There are so many remarkable nature beings that we often miss, as we do not take the time to recognize the smallest of beings. There are wondrous beings such as mosses, fungi, and insects that are so small we must walk slowly to discover them.

As you continue walking on the path, notice a building in a meadow in the distance that seems to glow. Once you approach, enter the door of the building, where a guardian spirit is waiting to cleanse you. Let this guardian spirit cleanse you so that you are only bringing peace, love, and light into your new altar room. The guardian spirit might use a feather to cleanse your field of energy or maybe some incense. Or the compassionate spirit might put a drop of water on your third eye or your crown as you let go of any burdens and any energy that needs to be released. The guardian spirit might whisper a message into your ear. Stay open to a unique cleansing method that this helping spirit might perform. Remember that this is being done so that you create a clear field of energy in the altar room where everyone is safe to fully open to the power of working in the unseen realms.

Once you are cleansed, enter the room. Notice that there is a gorgeous altar cloth on the floor. It is right in the middle of the room, big enough for your community to be able to stand or sit around. This altar cloth is woven with many vibrant colors. Some of them are ordinary colors, while some might be translucent nonordinary colors. You can feel the magic of the energy that they exude. There are threads of all different colors and textures woven together. This weaving of threads might remind you of the web of life. Gaze upon the lovely altar cloth. As you do this, notice the large crystal sculpture of the Earth on the altar.

There is incense burning, as well as candles of vibrant colors: green, red, yellow, blue, purple, lavender, silver, and gold. The burning candles remind you of the beauty of your spirit. There are offering bowls that have been filled with cornmeal, different healing herbs, rose petals, and lavender; and there are power objects of stones, branches, flowers, crystals, and exquisite offerings that honor nature as well as your connection with all that is alive. Some are in different bowls, and some are spread on top of the altar cloth.

As you continue to visit your altar room over the weeks or years to come (for this altar room will always exist outside of time), you can bring your own gifts. Some people leave on the altar special jewelry, flowers, stones, and crystals.

This is an altar room you can visit on your own at any time without the need to tell your friends, family, or community. It is a place you can visit alone by taking a shamanic journey or through meditation, to go and sit there for comfort, to pray, or to perform your own ceremonies in the invisible realms. There will also be times when your group visits the altar together to perform ceremonies when the need or desire exists.

You might even decide to send instructions for a ceremony that people in your family or community perform in the altar room in their own time when it is impossible to coordinate timing for everyone to join in the ceremony.

Experience your heartbeat and focus on blessing words. This is a blessing of love for yourself, your community, and all of life. You can say out loud words of gratitude, words of power to empower your circle. Or you can write the blessing words such as "grace," "peace," "love," "trust," and "gratitude" on paper and leave them in offering bowls on the altar.

You have begun creating your altar room, and it is now time to take your leave. Just before you leave, gaze at the stunning altar. Embrace and absorb the light of your circle if you came together as a group. This altar room is now a spiritual home and sanctuary for all of you.

It is now time to return. Leave through the entrance of the room. You might notice a guardian spirit blessing you as you leave.

Walk back down the path that you took to get to this glowing building. Notice your surroundings, the textures, the fragrances, the feelings, and the sounds. Return to the veil that you stepped through to enter into the unseen realms and step through it into your home and the room you are working in. Take some deep grounding breaths. Open your eyes. Feel yourself present.

As you feel yourself becoming present, notice if you have an inner smile from being in your special altar room and being in a glorious circle together with your group. Feel gratitude. You know in your heart and soul that as you continue to share with your circle, you will experience a wealth of love, power, and healing. You will receive this healing personally, and you can share it with the Earth and all of life. Let the helping spirits you called in know that your work is done for now. It is simply courtesy to let the compassionate spirits know that they can also take their leave.

Part Two

SACRED
TRANSITIONS

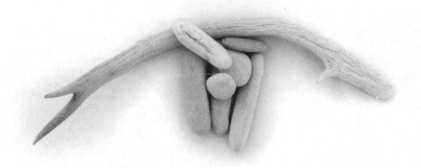

6

Turning Points
and Rites of Passage

Ceremonies have always been used to mark a change in a person's life. In shamanic cultures, each member of a community plays an important role in maintaining the health of the community at large. Each person is honored for the gifts and strengths they bring to the community, and when an individual experiences a change in life, they can then contribute new strengths, gifts, and talents. The community honors and welcomes back anyone who transitions into a new time of life.

In our culture, we forget that we all are connected to something bigger than ourselves—the Earth and nature, the web of life, and our communities. We can see how the health of our communities is failing as we have forgotten the power of embracing the contribution of individual gifts shared. It puts too much stress on the immune system of the community, the web of life, and the Earth when we do not share the energy that is needed to maintain a state of health.

A loving helping spirit once showed me how in today's world we act like disconnected body parts. A hand does not have a life of its own. We act as if we are all separate body parts living in isolation, which simply does not work.

You can certainly perform a ceremony to honor a transition, initiation, or rite of passage on your own. But there is a power of bringing in other people to perform a ceremony that marks a change in life, such as honoring a birth and the parents who will be changed by bringing a new life into the world. In rite of passage ceremonies, it is powerful to have other people witness and support a child moving into their teenage years or into adulthood.

Inviting others to honor these changes creates a powerful witnessing and provides support to the individual, couple, or family experiencing transition. If we learn to stop isolating ourselves, we rediscover the power of creating, living, and working in healthy communities.

Sometimes working in community can bring up concerns. There are some communities in which people are looking for a leader to control their lives, projecting the role of "the protective parent" onto them. As changes continue in the world, people move into states of anxiety and rally around beliefs of division, hate, and fear. These types of communities pull the collective apart instead of adding strength.

The Book of Ceremony is written for communities to come together in the spirit of love and unity to help each other and all of life. Yes, group dynamics come up. In doing your ceremonial work together, it is important to either deal with any disharmonious relationships in the circle or ask people to put aside their differences for now and step fully into a divine and sacred space of consciousness where love, light, and peace are the energies infusing your circle.

Shamans have always performed ceremonies for people to heal relationship issues so that the community can return to a state of harmony. Once you have finished reading *The Book of Ceremony*, you can journey or meditate on a ceremony to resolve challenging group dynamics in the circle of people who have gathered to work together.

When I teach online courses, the comments and feedback I receive reveal how much renewal and healing comes from gathering with others online to perform virtual ceremonies. The support and love of the circle makes it such a precious event. Many people come to realize this kind of support is a missing piece in living a joyful life. Being part of a supportive community of people who are praying for you during ceremony and holding space creates healing on its own, no matter what the nature of the ceremony is.

I find that many of the people who participate with me in these global nonordinary ceremonies go on to find local groups where they can continue their work. As wonderful as it is to have hundreds of people supporting you remotely, nothing can take the place of the bonding that occurs when joining together with friends and local communities in the physical. Both ways of working bring beauty and grace into your life and into the world.

In performing ceremonies where you invite friends, loved ones, and other members of the community, it is still important to perform preparation work to distinguish between a social gathering and a powerful ceremony to honor a transition. In most cases, not everyone present will embrace the practice of shamanism. Bring in elements that create sacred space so that the power of the universe participates in the ceremony. In this way, all who are present, no matter what religious or spiritual practice they follow, can focus on the spiritual intention of the event they are joining in. Intention is key in having the power of the universe participate in any healing or blessing that will take place.

We often bring gifts to celebrate a time of change—a birth, a wedding, a birthday, and so on. Gifts are wonderful and can help provide people with clothing, furnishings, or cooking utensils, and other needs, easing the financial burden that comes with moving into a new phase of life.

It is important to honor the fact that ceremonies go far beyond gift giving. In our modern world, our ceremonies can become too focused on the material and leave out the unseen power of what the transition or transformation is really about. As we bring in new ways to honor times of change, it helps individuals and families step into a new role in life.

In 2004 I had the remarkable opportunity to be part of a pilot research study with the University of Michigan's Integrative Medicine program. We were researching how some of the shamanic work I teach could help people who had suffered a heart attack. I led powerful healing ceremonies for the group, even though the majority of the group involved in my workshop were fundamentalist Christians. I could not talk about shamanism or helping spirits. Many in the group sat in class holding their Bibles.

I shared how the power of drumming produces hormones that alleviate stress. And I shared how singing and dancing assist in releasing burdening thoughts. No matter what our religious or spiritual beliefs are, we all have a sense that our ongoing mental chatter prevents us from fully participating in spiritual ceremonies. And we also know that finding ways to quiet our mind and relieve stress is good for our health.

We performed fire ceremonies to release old hurts and blessing ceremonies to pray for everyone's good health. And we performed the transfiguration ceremony that I will end *The Book of Ceremony* with. Two miraculous healings occurred from performing this one ceremony. The most amazing thing was to witness everyone's participation in the ceremonies as if they were in a shamanic circle. I wrote about performing transfiguration ceremonies on behalf of others in my book *Walking in Light*.

It is important if you are leading a ceremony to do your own preparation before working with your group. Find simple ways, such as opening with a prayer or a song, to bring people into sacred space. The time for "partying" is when the ceremony is over, and you can celebrate the powerful work that has been done.

When I lead ceremonies, sometimes I consult with my helping spirits to get the timing and the structure. If you practice shamanic journeying, I would suggest you use journeying as a tool to create your ceremony. I often just let my heart and intuition guide me. As long as you use the elements of ceremony and state an intention, your own intuition will provide you with ideas for the perfect ceremony.

WELCOMING A NEW BABY INTO THE WORLD

Welcoming a child into the world and blessing the parents is a powerful rite of passage. There are many ceremonies that you can perform as you honor this time in a family's life, as well as for the community at large. These include ceremonies for the pregnant mother, for the child's birth, and for loved ones who gather to welcome the baby into the world.

Here are some guidelines for ceremonies to support a pregnant mother. Invite other women who help prepare the mother for the transition in her life. Invite elders and women of all ages to share stories of life changes and support the mother in her new role. Elders can share stories of being parents and how meaningful and challenging this new role can be. Women can massage the hands or feet of the pregnant woman to put her at ease and allow her to feel the love and support surrounding her.

Following is an example of a ceremony for an expecting mother.

SUPPORTING MARIA IN HER FIRST PREGNANCY

When Maria was pregnant, she was a bit frightened by the responsibility of bringing a child into the world at such a turbulent time on the planet. She hadn't really processed all the ways a baby would impact her life. Maria found true comfort when her friends and family performed an honoring ceremony on her behalf.

Helena, a long-time student of shamanism, helped gather women from Maria's intimate community to come and stand strong with her as she prepared for welcoming her baby into the world. Everyone came ready to share funny and heartwarming experiences of giving birth and raising their children. They came with gifts that took on a deep meaning. The gifts were all imbued with love to bless a good birth and to honor a new child entering our exquisite Earth.

Some of Maria's friends brought incense to burn and massage oils. A couple of the women were wonderful crafters who wove willow branches into small nests. They put some soft moss inside, along with colorful candy eggs to represent the natural process of birth.

Once Helena performed an invocation to set the focus of the ceremony, it took on a life of its own. Helena greeted the family's helping ancestors and prayed for their assistance for a graceful and healthy birth. Maria felt embraced and surrounded by a wealth of care, love, and support—she cried tears of joy. She processed with others the joys and fears about this next phase of her life. The women present said loving words to the baby as they gently placed their hands on Maria's growing belly.

Music was played that held the focus of this being a sacred event instead of a party. The group celebrated with Maria's favorite foods and drinks, but again in a sacred and honoring way. The gifts given held prayers for good health and joy to support the newborn.

Once the baby was born, Helena gathered both male and female family members and friends for another ceremony to honor the baby and the parents. She shared how in past times it was understood that each child that was born brought creative gifts into the community that would help maintain harmony in community life. She shared the loss we feel in our modern life as we isolate ourselves from community and the importance of gathering to fully engage and support each other in times of joy, change, and challenges.

Helena spoke about how societies in the past recognized the blessings a new child would bring into the family and community and the importance of letting babies know that they are truly welcomed into the world.

Although babies and other life-forms in nature do not speak, they are still psychically sensitive to what is happening in their environment. Helena shared the idea that many people who feel a sense of being out of place in the world might have first experienced this disconnection because of a sterile birth experience in which they were not welcomed and honored in a sacred way. This lack of feeling welcomed can create feelings of unworthiness, a sense that we do not deserve the best that life has to offer, and an inability to bond with others.

Maria's welcoming ceremony was created to let her baby feel truly honored and embraced. It was created with the intention to give her baby a strong foundation for relating with others and feeling worthy on her journey through life.

Helena then led a simple ceremony where each person present had a turn in sharing the strengths and gifts they perceived that this baby would share with others. Each had a turn in saying blessings supporting this new life and the parents.

Maria and her husband, Roy, were so touched by these beautiful blessings for good health, joy, love, and strength that they seemed to glow. They felt the full support of their loved ones in raising this precious child, who will help the community evolve through her unique gifts.

The next step of the ceremony was a rite of passage to welcome Maria and Roy into their new role in the community. In bringing a new child into the world, they would be changed forever. An essential part of a rite of passage ceremony for anyone experiencing a transition is to welcome the initiates back into the community, as they are now changed and embody a new wisdom and presence.

Helena ended the ceremony by thanking everyone who attended, and she thanked the spiritual forces who were present to witness this sacred event. Then it was time to celebrate with gift giving, food and drinks, and more celebratory conversation.

Naming Ceremonies

In shamanic cultures, words are seen as magic and carry the vibration of our intent into the world. Our self-talk has the same power to affect our inner life.

The shamanic understanding about the power of words is true with our own names and the names we give children. In my own case, elders have taught me to use my given name, Sandra, instead of the nickname Sandy. The vibrations behind these two names hold a different frequency.

In a naming ceremony, one of the key parts of the preparation should be greeting and welcoming your helping ancestral spirits. They will be watching out for the child from when they are born until the time of death. During the ceremony, the name of a child is honored. The ceremonial leader strongly speaks the name out loud in front of a community, so everyone can hear the power of the new energy entering the field of the collective.

A naming ceremony for a child can easily be a part of the welcoming ceremony I described above, or it can be its own distinct ceremony.

Another type of naming in shamanic cultures is to give a spiritual name. For a child, this name represents the gifts and talents they would bring to the community, such as "She Who Shines," "He Who Crafts," "He Who Dreams," and "She Who Knows."

Spiritual names can take on many forms and can be adopted at any point in life to honor a transition or a new direction. I have students who take a spiritual name for themselves after embracing a spiritual practice, such as "River Flow," "Tree Woman," or "Sunshine." The ceremony of taking a spiritual name is a way to honor a new energy that will become a guiding part of your identity.

In the early 1980s, I attended a vision quest and sweat lodge ceremony led by a Native American elder. During our time together, I had shared how much I love trees. At sunrise, the sunlight beamed through the door of the sweat lodge onto my heart center. The elder saw that I was blessed by the sun, and he stood up and gave me the name "Little Sister" to reflect my deep relationship with the trees and to honor my deeply felt connection with them as part of my family.

The easiest way to perform such a ceremony is to have others honor the name you have chosen. You can also perform a naming ceremony for yourself by spending time in nature. Prepare and invoke the helping spirits. You might drum or rattle to begin. State your intention out loud, so all beings in nature and in the unseen worlds can hear you say, "I now go by the name 'She Who Brings Peace.'" After stating your name out loud, reflect in silence on the new energy you are sharing with the world, your community, and all of life. Be confident in standing strong in your new name and the gifts you will now share with the web of life.

Leave some offerings on the land. When you feel done, state out loud, "The work is done for now." You have now entered a new phase of your life where you commit to being a person who reflects back vital qualities that are needed for the health of all in the web of life. Improvise on the ceremony that I have described to make it your own.

Rites of Passage

In shamanic cultures, it is part of community life to create a rite of passage ceremony for a child transitioning from childhood to adolescence to adulthood. These are also known as "coming of age" ceremonies.

Some of the familiar modern ways we acknowledge such rites of passage are coming of age parties, debutante balls, and the bar mitzvah or bat mitzvah of Jewish tradition to mark a boy's becoming a man or a girl becoming a woman. Sweet 16 parties are celebrations welcoming a girl into her womanhood. There are numerous names used in different religious and spiritual cultures for rites of passage.

It is important to use sacred ceremony to honor a child entering into adulthood. It helps them navigate childhood to adolescence and then to adulthood as they wrestle with the role of who they are and want to be.

Typically, in a shamanic culture, it is up to the elders to oversee the rite of passage ceremony. There is usually a period of time when the child or group of children is separated from the community while they are educated by elders about the importance of stepping into the role of a responsible adult who will help the community thrive. The elders prepare them for their rite of passage ceremony.

Children are often given a physical test. They might go on a vision quest, fast, and pray for a vision that will prepare them for their rite of passage. In some cultures, the tests were or are still quite intense or even perilous. Initiates might walk through fire, be buried in the earth, or sit in a darkened cave for days or weeks. Such rites caused initiates to have to rely on the strength of their spirit instead of willpower to survive the life-changing event. Once the child learned about the strength of their own spiritual nature, they were deemed ready to take on the role of an adult.

If we do not lead powerful rite of passage ceremonies today, young adults often join gangs where they can participate in acts that endanger their lives. They do this hoping to feel like an adult and to feel like they belong to a community that understands what they are going through.

The immense modern issue of bullying in schools is a reflection of the need to have rites of passage where each child is honored and knows their role in the community.

Without a rite of passage ceremony into adolescence, some children feel lost, awkward, and that they do not belong. They may turn to drugs or alcohol. In the worst cases, they become suicidal or start to act out violently against others, having lost sight of the preciousness of life. This impacts the child, their family, and the community at large. The statistics of teens committing suicide are quite alarming. It is time to give our young adults the gift of learning about how the strength of their spirit can support them through life's challenges instead of only teaching them how to power through. It is time to help our children learn about their authentic identity.

Today, there are many reputable organizations that lead vision quests for young adults. In a vision quest, participants sit in nature, often fasting and praying for a vision. There are also organizations that responsibly create a survival experience. Once the teens get into nature and learn how to survive on their own, where they have to build their own shelter and find food and water, something changes within them. They develop an adult's confidence in their inner strength. This process has been very successful with troubled teens.

We must adapt ancient ceremonies to fit the times and culture we live in. Children and teens must always be kept safe during any rite of passage. To honor a child's transformation into an adult is the most empowering part of a rite of passage. The key to any initiation ceremony is helping a child find their spiritual strength, which is the true force that carries them through the challenging and turbulent times that are part of life.

Leading vision quests and survival quests in nature is beyond the scope of this book, but you can improvise on creating rite of passage ceremonies. Arranging a long backpacking trip that your child might be interested in is a perfect way to help your child mature. Another kind of nature adventure, such as a long river-rafting trip or mountain climbing, can also bring in a new understanding of life as an adult and the desire to take on new responsibilities. You might consider a pilgrimage, such as traveling abroad alone, that the teen takes to mark the new transition in their life.

Sharing stories of your ancestry with your children will also give them a feeling of connecting to an ancestral lineage beyond themselves and their immediate family.

ROSE'S RITE OF PASSAGE CEREMONY

Jacqueline wanted to create a rite of passage ceremony for her daughter Rose. On Rose's thirteenth birthday, Jacqueline invited friends, family members, and elders in her community to participate and witness Rose being honored into the next phase of her life.

Jacqueline decorated her backyard with a huge arbor created by long branches filled with stunning, fragrant roses honoring her daughter's name. Other community members helped Jacqueline gather materials for the arbor. They also contributed food and drinks for the celebration afterward.

When the day came for the rite of passage ceremony, Jacqueline was quite nervous. She did her preparation work and set her intention. Jacqueline greeted her ancestral lineage to witness and support Rose's coming of age ceremony. She had written down an invocation, as she feared no words would emerge when it was time for her to speak. Yet she found that once everyone gathered, and Rose appeared wearing an exquisite dress, the words just gracefully flowed.

After the invocation was stated, the gathered women began telling Rose stories about their lives, including what their childhoods were like and what they experienced as they passed through puberty. They shared stories about how awkward they felt with the changes in their bodies, and they shared funny stories about meeting boys. They talked about what they wished they had known when they were thirteen.

Rose sat in the center of the group soaking in all the love and stories with a smile on her face. There was a lot of joy and giggling going on in the room.

Once the storytelling was done, Jacqueline went up and kissed Rose on the cheek. She tenderly shared with Rose that she loved raising her. She now looked forward to welcoming Rose into her womanhood, witnessing and supporting her as she dated, fell in love, chose a career, celebrated her own marriage, and birthed a child. This, of course, was if Rose chose to marry and/or have children.

Rose was led to the sacred arbor Jacqueline had created with great love and attention. All the gathered women stood on the other side of the arbor.

Jacqueline again kissed her daughter on her cheek and stated out loud, "You now walk from being a child into becoming a beautiful woman." Rose walked through the arbor that symbolized a transition of one time of life to another. As she walked through, the women shared words of empowerment, strength, and encouragement. As Rose exited the arbor, she was welcomed by all the women as a peer and woman who was now in a new phase of life. Rose looked radiant.

Jacqueline thanked the helping spirits for witnessing this powerful rite of passage honoring her daughter. Jacqueline said that the spiritual ceremony had ended, and it was now time to celebrate.

Rose was obviously touched by all that occurred. She felt different. She knew she had entered a new phase of life. She also recognized that it would take her time to process what all of this meant. She appreciated the ceremony and felt it helped her to navigate from feeling like a child to feeling like a woman.

JASON'S RITE OF PASSAGE

Jason was struggling in school. He was having a lot of problems when he moved into puberty. He lost his ability to concentrate on his schoolwork and felt awkward socially. His parents worried that he was not bonding with his schoolmates and was becoming withdrawn.

Jason's father, Steve, understood the importance of a rite of passage ceremony. He knew this would help to bring Jason out. Jason agreed to go on a five-day backpacking trip with his dad. Jason was responsible for setting up camp and cooking the food. Steve would sit with Jason as he performed his duties.

Both father and son pushed their bodies beyond what they felt they were capable of and discovered the reservoir of their inner strength while traveling through nature with no electronic devices or other distractions to keep them anchored to their ordinary life.

They had long talks as they sat around the fire at night. This was a time when Steve spoke about his awkwardness when he was a boy, and how his grandfather and father had imparted wisdom to help him understand what he was going through. He shared with candor and vulnerability what it was like for him to eventually move from his challenging boyhood into becoming a successful businessman, a loving father and husband, and an engaged member of his community.

Jason opened up about the challenges he was facing during his teenage years, creating a new relationship in being able to talk to his father as one man to another. To add another element of sweetness in this coming of age ceremony, Steve taught Jason how to shave.

Steve ended the ceremony by anointing Jason with the ash from the coals of the fire that burned all night. It was a symbolic act, representing that Jason had now moved into a new phase of life.

Although there was no drumming or rattling as part of their time together, this is a classic rite of passage ceremony for a boy. In adapting this ceremony, you could easily introduce drumming in nature as a component of this rite to welcome a boy into becoming a man.

For Jason, this ceremony did transform his life and the challenges he faced. He learned he had more survival skills than he had imagined, which gave him confidence. Jason felt that he could take on more responsibility, that he was worthy to have friends and be accepted by his schoolmates, and he felt a change in his own presence and stature as he walked back down the long trail.

Remember that a very important phase of any rite of passage ceremony is the reintegration process back into the community. Once home, Jason was greeted by friends and family members standing together in a circle in the garden. Each person welcomed Jason back home and shared inspiring words. The ceremony ended with Jason's father playing the guitar and singing a song he chose to welcome Jason into adulthood. Then they celebrated with a delicious meal.

OTHER RITE OF PASSAGE CEREMONIES

Ceremonies can be created not just to honor the change that comes with puberty. Use your imagination to create ceremonies to honor someone who gets a driver's license, graduates from high school, graduates from college, gets their first job, and so on. There are the rites of passage marking transitions from maiden to mother to crone. We go through a rite of passage at middle age.

Another time of deep inner change is when we lose both of our parents. In some cases, people feel that they have truly moved into adulthood after feeling they are now "orphans." When we move into our elder years, we go through a rite of passage as we begin to let go of the material world and withdraw to create a deep inner life. Improvising and using the structure described in part 1 will assist you in creating ceremonies that honor these transitions.

SACRED MARRIAGES

Our culture puts a lot of pressure on couples to plan a "perfect" wedding to honor their love. Creating a big wedding can put a couple or family under financial stress. Issues come up about whom to invite, what to serve, what to wear, and the list goes on. Many people are choosing simpler wedding ceremonies today that focus on the true meaning of marriage instead of lavish celebrations that can lead to financial debt and rifts in families.

My husband, Woods, and I lived together for years before getting married. We wanted to perform our own shamanic wedding and leave out the legalities. We felt that the commitment of getting married with spirit as our witness was more binding than a legal document.

We live in the country, and we went out onto our land. It was a snowy, cold winter's day. Wearing snow boots, we hiked down to an artesian spring covered with snow. The white snow next to the green pine, juniper, and ponderosa trees created a magical atmosphere along with complete silence on the land.

I rattled to call in, greet, and welcome the spirit of the land, the helping ancestors, the spirit of Santa Fe, our helping spirits, and our own ancestors. I stated my invocation out loud, thanking the elements of earth, air, water, and fire (as the sun), and all the beings in nature for witnessing our commitment ceremony. Woods and I took turns expressing our love for each other and then exchanged wedding rings. We left two red roses on the snow covering the spring. We thanked the spirits and closed our ceremony. It was a precious experience for both of us, and we felt truly committed to each other.

We took some photos of each other and of the trees witnessing this sacred event. The photos showed luminous blue orbs in the juniper trees. This was a sign that we were truly blessed and supported.

Years later, we wanted to make our marriage legal. I asked a friend who embraced the practice of shamanism to be our minister. We invited a small group of dear friends to come and be part of the rite of passage of getting legally married.

Once again, we chose winter as the time to perform our ceremony. And it was again snowing, so we asked our guests to dress for the snow and the cold.

Katherine, our minister, did a lovely job invoking the spirits. We stood in a circle on our snow-covered deck, appreciating the beauty of the bright sunlight making the snow shimmer. Katherine asked each person to recount a funny or touching experience about me and Woods. There was a lot of laughter. Our friends reached into their hearts and shared stories that expressed their love and support.

After everyone shared a memorable story, Woods and I spoke to each other from our heart about our love and what our relationship meant to us. We then exchanged the same rings again, and Katherine pronounced us husband and wife.

After Katherine closed the ceremony, we all shared food and drink together.

It was such a sweet and intimate ceremony. Everyone left feeling that they had participated in a spiritual experience that had deep meaning for all.

I am sharing my experience with you to give you some ideas of how you can improvise a wedding ceremony if you don't go the traditional route of creating a huge event where you have a hundred or more guests.

There are couples and families who do want to have a large celebration of people witnessing their love and commitment to each other. You can certainly create a sacred ceremony at a large wedding by greeting the compassionate spirits and bringing everyone together with the correct focus. Be clear that the wedding is more than a party—it is a sacred event that has deep meaning. Whether a ceremony is used to honor the sacred marriage of a heterosexual relationship or a same-sex relationship would not change a shamanic marriage ceremony.

Weddings honor love and commitment. It is beautiful when a couple stands in the presence of loved ones, the helping spirits, and the divine, all witnessing and supporting the intention of the ceremony.

Inviting a minister with a shamanic background can provide a powerful way to weave through spiritual words that are an invocation inviting the divine to bear witness. Ask guests to step into a place of honor and respect for the couple during the invocation and ceremony. Ask them to feed wishes for good health and continued love through both good and challenging times. These steps bring a spiritual aspect to any wedding ceremony you wish to design.

Invite close friends and relatives to share short, funny stories in an honoring way. The entire wealth of guests can join in with blessings, love, and laughter.

Place a bowl of crystal hearts on a table and ask all the guests to blow wishes for the couple into the crystals. In this way, the bowl of crystals can sit in the new couple's home radiating beneficial wishes for the goodness of life. Instead of crystals, you can collect stones or place rose petals in a bowl. Ask everyone to state out loud a one-word blessing that surrounds and "rains down" on a couple while they drink their favorite drink together toasting their love. These are simple, sacred ways of adding to the usual toasts given at a wedding.

When performing a wedding outside, such as in a park or at a beach, consider including an arbor in the ceremony. These can be simply built and lined with candles, decorations, vines, and flowers. Perform an invocation, and then invite the couple to walk through the arbor from a place of separation to togetherness. This is a powerful ceremonial element that can fit into any marriage, large or small.

The key is to weave in spiritual phrases, invocations, and acts to honor and bless the couple. You can easily transform any wedding ceremony from a party into a true spiritual celebration.

It is never too late to perform a "recommitment" ceremony with your spouse if you felt that your initial wedding celebration did not carry a strong sacred energy. You can even perform such a recommitment ceremony on an anniversary. This can revitalize a marriage and refuel the depth of your commitment and love for each other.

7

HONORABLE CLOSURE

We all go through transitions that involve leaving a relationship, changing jobs, moving, or saying goodbye to a loved one who has passed away.

In the early 1980s, I studied tarot with Angeles Arrien, who was a brilliant cross-cultural anthropologist. I was having an issue with leaving a relationship that no longer felt healthy for me. The ending of the relationship was not mutually desired, and it was difficult to break my connection with my partner.

I spoke to Angeles, and she taught me about the importance of performing a ceremony of honorable closure. In this ceremony, both people say what they need to say to each other, and then the door is closed to future conversations so that each person can move on. If it is not possible to meet or talk with the other person in the relationship, then this can be a one-sided conversation. The ceremony releases the restrictive energetic bonds in a relationship, allowing both people to move on.

I've learned a lot over the years about honorable closure. Sometimes a ceremony needs to be performed to close the door to future conversations. But people who break up can become good friends by dissolving the unhealthy energetic ties that bind them together. A ceremony can help people move their relationship gracefully from being lovers to being friends.

Most of us carry childhood wounds. These wounds are like seeds planted in our inner garden, which grow as we age. If we are unaware of these wounds, we might attract people in our lives who reflect back to us a quality or wound we still have to heal. As we choose to work on ourselves through spiritual practice and ceremony, we can evolve and heal. We can begin to dissolve links to people who reflect our wounds and attract people into our lives who reflect a state of emotional health. This process might involve ending your energetic connection with a person you have grown away from. Or you both might work on creating a new, strong, and healthy relationship, where you mirror and reinforce your strengths and self-love.

Staying in an unhealthy relationship is like throwing an anchor down to your past. Such relationships can prevent you from moving forward to new life situations and attracting relationships that reflect the person you have become. In shamanic cultures, this is seen as the need to break energetic cords, strings, or threads that keep you from moving forward to a new phase in life.

We do not want to be burdened by our past. The energy of the past can create so much weight on our body and emotions that we cannot truly move on to create a healthy present and future. As much as we desire healthier and more meaningful relationships, we often end up trapped, creating the same situations over and over. The faces might change, but the story remains the same.

There comes a time in our own growth and evolution when we must let go of the ties that bind us to our past, whether it means leaving a job, a place, or a relationship. We must leave the old behind while carrying the good memories and life lessons. We all want the freedom to create beneficial relationships and life circumstances that bring us new opportunities for growth. We cannot do this while we hang on to the past. That's why ceremonies that provide us with honorable closure are such a powerful tool for healing.

RELEASING AND TRANSFORMING UNHEALTHY RELATIONSHIPS

Here is guidance for an unwinding ceremony you can perform before, during, or after ending a relationship with a partner, a friend, or even a coworker.

Visit a place in nature and spend time processing the feelings that your relationship brings up for you. Prepare and greet the helping spirits or spiritual forces you wish to engage in the unwinding act. State out loud or in silence that you are grateful for all the lessons you received in your relationship but that it is now time to move on.

Allow any emotions that emerge to flow so that you do not blindly move into a place of anger or hurt when you are ready to do your unwinding ceremony. When you consciously process your anger, feelings of hurt, or any trauma associated with the ending of the relationship, you step into a place of empowerment, and you will have more success with performing your ceremony.

Invite one or two friends who support you and can hold the space for you, or you can experience the power of working alone. Decide what you personally need. Some people might feel awkward processing emotions with others, while other people feel supported by it. We all have unique needs, and it is important to honor what feels right to you.

Once you have received clarity that you are ready to release the ties that bind you, gather your materials and design your ceremony. Feel free to adapt this guidance to make the ceremony your own.

Walk the land and find a stick to use in your ceremony. Keep your ceremony simple and drum, rattle, dance, and/or sing as you focus on your intention to release all ties to your unhealthy relationship. When you feel that you are in full connection with your soul through your preparation work and that you have the helping spirits or the divine forces you work with witnessing you, it is time to break the stick. This signifies honorable closure with the person you wish to be released from. End by leaving an offering on the land and thanking the helping spirits who witnessed your work.

This can also be done as a spontaneous ceremony when you are taking a walk in nature and feel intuitively guided to break an unhealthy energetic connection.

If you have friends with you, thank them for their support. Take some time to reflect on how you are feeling. You might still need to do some processing over time, but you should feel some relief and that a weight has been lifted from you.

JEREMIAH'S CEREMONY TO BURY HIS WEDDING RING

Jeremiah wanted a divorce from a woman he felt did not support his spiritual path and had no confidence in him. Their marriage had moved into an unhealthy place where there was no love. The connection between them became an obligation for both, and they were simply in a habit of being together. His wife was willing to stay in the relationship even though she wasn't happy. She felt safe and did not want to live alone.

Jeremiah came to see me as a client, processed all his feelings, and was ready to move into honorable closure. I spoke to Jeremiah about the power of ceremony in ending an unhealthy relationship and gave him some simple examples of how we could perform the ceremony.

Jeremiah decided what felt right for him to do. He asked me to be present and to drum for him.

Jeremiah buried his wedding ring in the earth, stating in a strong voice that this relationship was complete and over. He asked to be freed from the energy of his connection with his wife, now and for lifetimes to come.

I stood behind Jeremiah with my drum, giving him enough space to feel supported but also free to move and feel his own power.

When Jeremiah was done, he felt a sense of relief. He'd desired freedom from his wife for so long. He brushed the soil from his hands and reached into his pocket where he had some sacred herbs to leave for the earth.

After leaving his offerings, he turned away from the burial place under a magnificent old cottonwood tree, which was also witnessing this healing ceremony. He started to walk away. I thanked the helping spirits we had called in and had to hurry to catch up with Jeremiah, who was walking at a fast pace. He felt that part of his honorable closure was to finish the ceremony and never look back.

JUDY'S CEREMONY FOR AN AMICABLE DIVORCE

In Judy's case, she knew there was going to be a lot of conflict with her divorce. She understood that spiritually she could break a stick, bury a ring, or blow the energy of her relationship into a stone and place the stone in a river or in the ocean near where she lived. But she knew that she was going to face a complicated court battle involving the custody of her children.

Judy needed a ceremony to ask for the help of the universe to create an amenable court experience. She wished everyone involved could set aside their bitterness and make decisions to support the best interest of both partners and the children.

I consulted with Judy to help her design a ceremony. Judy loved the idea of working with fire to transform her emotions and carry her prayers up to the creative forces of the universe. She invited friends to help build a small fire on the beach in an isolated cove. They consulted together and decided to work on a night when the moon was full. The group loved the idea of drumming, rattling, dancing, and singing in the moonlight.

Judy prepared for the ceremony by creating two effigies. The first effigy was imbued with the emotions she wanted to release into the fire. The second represented a good result from the divorce hearing that would be for the highest good for all concerned, especially the children. Judy dreaded a bitter and ugly court scene. There was once love in the marriage, and she wanted an ending that honored and respected all she and her husband had built together.

Judy put special care into this second effigy. She walked in a park with offerings to find exquisite burnable objects in nature. As she found a flower, twig, or branch to use, she asked permission before taking each object. She used yarn to tie her effigy together. When completed, it looked like a little home that represented her old life, ready to be dissolved and transmuted by the fire. While making the effigy, she focused on the intention for the divorce hearing, praying that the bitter feelings would not override a healthy decision. She trusted that the universe would support her decision.

As the group gathered for the ceremony, everyone felt empowered by the fire, the ocean, and the moon. Each participant began calling in loving and compassionate spiritual forces to witness the work. They danced, sang, and drummed.

When the time was right, Judy called for a pause in the dancing to place her first effigy into the fire while her friends cheered her on. After more dancing and singing, Judy placed her second effigy in the fire, stating in a loud, clear voice what she was asking for during the divorce proceedings.

After ending the ceremony, Judy and her friends stayed up all night watching the fire burn, gazing at the beauty of the night sky, and listening to the beautiful and comforting sound of ocean waves. They shared great love stories, cried and laughed together, and spoke about their hopes and dreams.

The story ended well. Judy's husband had come to terms with the divorce by the time the hearing was set. The divorce was amicable, and joint custody of the children was established, which both parents felt was best for the children.

CONSTANCE'S CEREMONY TO HEAL AN ISSUE WITH A COWORKER

Constance worked at a job where her boss never supported her suggestions and basically made her life miserable at work. When we talked, I asked her to consider how people in our lives can reflect our own unresolved shadow material. Constance took time to meditate on how her boss mirrored back her own inability to love herself and be supportive of her decisions. She decided to perform a ceremony to release the energies she was projecting onto her boss.

Constance wrote these shadow qualities on paper to be burned. She watched the ashes float away into the air, representing a release of these projections. She thanked the air for transforming the energy she released into love and light, and she thanked the wind for sharing love with all of life and the Earth.

Before returning to her job, Constance performed a ceremony at home, stating to the universe a better vision of her experience at work. She gathered supplies, crafted images of loving and smiling people, and placed them on her altar. She wrote stories about being honored and respected for the good decisions she made in helping the business thrive. She performed hours of meditation, traveling within her inner landscape to her core to tap into self-love and self-respect while imagining how she wanted to be treated at work.

Once she returned to work, she was met by her boss's usual scowl. Constance placed her hands on her heart and breathed deeply. Suddenly her boss's expression softened, and the conversation shifted from the usual judgments to a casual discussion about how their weekends went. Although surprised by this sudden shift in behavior, Constance was thrilled and learned to trust herself, her spiritual work, and the universe to provide needed support.

Constance achieved closure and was able to stay at her job by transforming her relationship.

These are multiple ceremonies that can be performed for honorable closure. Journey, meditate, or spend time in nature to design your own.

Such ceremonies can bring surprising results. An unhealthy energetic connection with another person might cause them to need space and to break off all communication. This is usually an unconscious act, where people are not aware of the root cause of their not wanting to communicate. Once a ceremony for honorable closure is performed, someone who felt smothered by an unhealthy energetic connection, like a child who is estranged from their family, might pick up a phone after years of silence and simply say, "I was thinking about you and wanted to call." I have seen these shifts happen multiple times.

Death Is Not an End—It Is a Transition

In shamanic cultures, it is understood that death is a rite of passage as we move on to a new phase in our soul's journey. For this reason, death is not feared as it is for so many living in our world today.

Ceremonies to honor the deceased come in many forms, including celebrating the life of the deceased while recognizing the grief of the loved ones left.

I lead many memorials. It's a practice I've come to love. So much healing and closure can happen at a memorial led in a ceremonial way. This does not mean there is not more grieving to do, but having a sense of closure brings healing to loved ones, friends, and the community.

From a shamanic point of view, we are born into this life on Earth to live in a human body and experience life with our full senses; to learn about love; to create beauty, health, and peace; and to learn many other lessons. This is a place where we can evolve.

When a person dies, Earth is no longer their home. Their home is back to Source.

This does not mean when we perform a ceremony honoring a loved one's journey back to Source that we are trying to erase their memory. On the contrary, we continue to stay connected spiritually. A deceased loved one might become a helping spirit for a descendant. But Earth is for the living, and journeying home to Source is for the deceased. This journey is what we acknowledge during an honorable closure ceremony.

Guidelines for a Memorial Ceremony

Before the ceremony begins, I find out if a loved one has special needs. Sometimes a grieving loved one wants to tell the first funny story or memory, or to speak from their heart. Or they might just want to absorb all the love without needing to speak. I work with ceremonies that cater to individual needs.

If the community embraces shamanism, I call in the helping spirits and honor the directions. For a group with varied religious and spiritual beliefs, I use wording that fits with everyone's beliefs.

Everyone present stands in a circle. Each person in turn tells a funny or touching story, or recounts a memory about their deceased loved one. With a large group, I have to get "compassionately pushy" and be strict with my timing on how long people speak. If the stories go on too long, participants will get tired and distracted, and the power of the ceremony will diminish. I give people just a minute or two to speak.

Once the sharing is complete, I start drumming. I instruct everyone to close their eyes and focus on the deceased loved one. When ready, I ask everyone to raise their hands high into the air as they break their energetic connection, and let the deceased loved one go while wishing them a graceful and beautiful journey home. I drum until everyone has brought their hands back down.

I have performed this ceremony so many times, with shamanic groups and also with diverse religious groups. I always receive wonderful feedback on how touched everyone was by the ceremony and how it was exactly what they needed. The ceremony always creates lots of laughing and crying, but also a sense of closure. Everyone keeps their loving memories of the deceased while letting go of energetic bonds. This creates healing on many levels.

ROCHELLE'S SUICIDE MEMORIAL

I led one ceremony for a group of five friends. Rochelle, a dear friend of ours, had committed suicide. She was one of the kindest and most generous women we had met. We were in grief and shock. We knew she was struggling and in a lot of pain, but she'd never talked about ending her own life.

I brought balls of yarn, and we created an effigy of our friend. We tied yarn from the effigy to each of us. After each of us shared a wonderful story or memory of our friend, we cut each strand of yarn with scissors, representing that we were all letting her go to the light. This is an example of cutting energetic cords that might bind people together in an unhealthy fashion.

Blowing Bubbles of Love

I sometimes use bubbles that I buy at a toy store for group ceremonial work to wish a loved one a good journey home that is filled with grace, love, and light. There is great healing that comes from bringing an element of joy into a ceremony where people are grieving a loss.

I led a memorial ceremony for my mother, but I also performed a ceremony at her funeral. I kept it very simple. I talked about my mom and how much I loved her. I spoke about her life and what she contributed to me, her family, and the world by her presence. And then I asked all who were present to stand up and lift their arms to wish her a good journey home. We then blew bubbles toward the sky as we continued our prayers for her and remembered the joy she had brought into our lives.

Adaptations for Honoring Death

You can use adaptations and improvise on the ceremonies I've shared to honor the death of a pet, an animal from the wild, a species that has died en masse, a tree, a plant, and so on. Every living being on the planet should be honored while it is alive and once it transitions.

Burying a Pet

If you perform a burial ceremony for a beloved pet, you can place food and maybe a bit of water or milk in the grave. Share words of love for this precious animal who was a family member. Then raise your arms while wishing your pet a loving journey home that is filled with light, love, grace, and ease.

Plant Ceremony

I don't have a green thumb, but I love plants and grow many.

I actually created a plant graveyard on an isolated part of my land. I take a deceased plant to the graveyard. I thank it for sharing its beauty in my home and on the Earth and wish it a good journey home. I apologize for anything that I did that did not support its life by overwatering or not being able to provide optimal growing conditions. I leave offerings of blue corn meal.

I visit my plant graveyard frequently to pay my respects. Yes, I am a bit of an eccentric.

Honoring Trees

When a tree dies on my property, I visit with it. I thank it for the beauty and grace that it shared with all of life on this great Earth, while wishing it a good journey home. I leave an offering of blue corn meal in honor of its life.

I have received quite a bit of correspondence from people who were once loggers. They feel so much guilt about killing stately and oftentimes ancient trees. I share the ceremony I perform for my trees. You can perform the same ceremony for a mountainside where logging has occurred. You might not be able to talk to each tree individually, but you can stand in the affected area.

After preparing, say what is in your heart to the deceased trees, even if they have been removed. Drum, rattle, sing, and/or dance while praying in your own way that the trees have a good journey home. Thank them for their beautiful and powerful presence on the Earth. Leave heartfelt offerings. This same ceremony can be performed for trees lost in a blight or during a forest fire.

Honoring Environmental Losses

There are sad events that we are witnessing in which many die due to pollution in the land, air, and water where they live or during an environmental disaster. Climate change and war have created tragic situations for humans and all living beings. Floods, fires, earthquakes, tornadoes, and other disasters can force living beings to flee their homes or lose their lives. Even more heartbreaking is the mass extinction of so many precious species that could no longer survive in their natural environment.

There is such a power in performing ceremonies for living beings who have suffered devastation, whether these are human communities, animal and plant populations, or species lost to extinction.

You can perform a ceremony inside or outside to honor those who died. Thank them for the energetic signature they shared with the web of life and the beauty and preciousness they brought to the Earth. Say what is in your heart. Drum, rattle, sing, or perform your ceremony in silence as you honor the beings that have transitioned.

Since these are issues that affect us as a global community, you may find many people who want to join you. Performing local ceremonies or global virtual ceremonies helps us honor the lives lost and create a graceful journey home back to Source.

Virtual Ceremonies for Honorable Closure

A powerful way to work with closure ceremonies is to use the virtual altar that I suggested you create in chapter 5. Travel to the altar room alone or with a group. You can bring your group together remotely by phone or online. The leader should do most of the speaking in the ceremony, since cross talk is even more disruptive over electronic connections.

Lead the group to the altar room using a path as I suggested in the guided meditation. Be cleansed by the guardian spirits while leaving your ordinary thoughts and burdens behind. Gather at the altar cloth and greet each other. You might use a shamanic instrument and sing and dance to begin and end your ceremony.

Take turns sharing words and feelings. Once the sharing is complete, reach your arms up to the sky and wish the remarkable beings who have transitioned a good journey home. Thank the helping spirits.

Travel home. Take time to share your experience of doing this potent and heartwarming work. Some members of the group might have received spiritual messages of love to share from the beings you honored.

Spontaneous Ceremonies

You might witness an accident or another traumatic event or come across the body of a deceased animal. Many shamanic practitioners carry offerings in their car or on their person for such an event. At the scene of an accident, say a prayer for those impacted and leave an offering on the land. With a creature found dead on the road or while walking in nature, you might say prayers of honor and respect for its life and for gracing this Earth with its presence, leave an offering, and even bury it in a ceremonial way if the situation allows.

While grieving any death, we often feel heartbroken. Though this is painful, it gives our hearts the opportunity to open, expand, and embrace more compassion.

Honoring Grief

In shamanic cultures, ceremonies are performed to honor the transition of a community member. But ceremonies can also serve to honor the grief of loved ones. Grief has its own process. We go through different phases of grief. Ceremonies might not heal grief immediately, but they can begin a process that is an important passage in life.

All of life grieves. Even animals, trees, plants, birds, and other beings grieve the death of a partner. Each individual's grief has its own time frame. Whether it takes days, months, or years to heal from grief, honoring the process through ceremony can help us through each step of the journey.

DEBORAH'S DANCE OF GRIEF

Deborah decided to perform a ceremony to honor the loss of a dear friend. She invited friends to work at night around a fire. They gathered their materials, prepared, and called in the goddess energies to support their dance of grief. They took turns drumming and singing to hold the space while small groups of women traveled within themselves to feel their heartbreak of losing a friend. They danced whatever emotion emerged for them.

They took turns dancing for hours until their tears ended. They all felt held in love while expressing their emotions. Though each knew they had more grieving to do, they felt stronger and more prepared to cope with the days ahead.

On the Need for Strong Communities

In shamanic cultures, community members know each other well. They understand the need to listen to those in the community who suffer during a war, a tragedy, or a mental or emotional breakdown.

The community knows how to listen, hold the hurt community member in love, and welcome them home after suffering trauma.

In *Walking in Light*, I address in depth the tragedies we are facing due to the lack of strong and supportive communities. We need to create strength in our communities so that we can embrace the home-coming of our initiates instead of leaving them to feel estranged and isolated. We can accomplish this through the power of ceremony.

Part Three

CEREMONIES TO CREATE ENERGETIC BALANCE

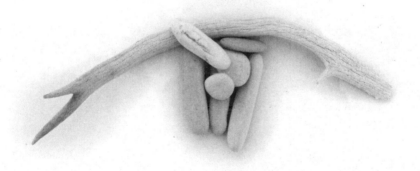

8

RELEASING
BLOCKING ENERGIES

We have the opportunity to bring the sacred to all areas of our lives. Sometimes we need to find the right time and place to perform a ceremony that honors a transition, whether it is joyful or challenging. When we integrate the sacredness of ceremony into our daily activities, we create true change in our personal lives as well as for all of life.

As I have already shared, all beings contribute an energetic signature to the web of life. We can think of this as just a mental concept, but we can only truly experience this connection when we open ourselves to the felt sense of connection, a shared frequency of energy with all of existence.

The web of life is an organism that contains the energy you bring to it. Whenever you engage in healing, feeling the bliss and preciousness of life, or maintaining a discipline of being mindful with the energy of your words and thoughts, you shift the vibration of the web. It is amazing to take some time to journey and meditate, so you can feel this connection at a level deeper than rational understanding.

Exercise to Feel the Vibration
in the Web of Life

Imagine traveling within your body and experiencing
a shimmering web connecting all of your cells, organs,
and body parts. The silklike threads of the web are
finely tuned, like those of an exquisitely made stringed
instrument. Let the frequency of your favorite word
vibrate throughout this inner web. Notice how it feels.
Let a joyful thought vibrate through this web and
observe how it impacts your cells.

The web that lives inside you is the same web that
connects all of life in the outer world. Continue to
explore how your thoughts and words affect yourself
and the web of life.

We tend to separate spiritual practices from our ordinary daily
activities. We might meditate in the morning and do exercises to
strengthen our body, mind, and spirit—walking, jogging, yoga, tai
chi, qigong, and so on. Then we leave behind all the wonderful
energy generated and dive in to the stress and distractions of ordinary living. By integrating spiritual energies, we can become a source
of light for ourselves, our loved ones, the community we interact
with, and the planet.

LET IT GO

There are engaging ceremonies we can perform to bless our home,
garden, land, loved ones, and all of life. Yet since the outer world is a
reflection of our inner state of consciousness, our work to honor and
bless our outer environment will only succeed if we release destructive
patterns, such as these:

- Sabotaging thoughts

- Old hurts

- Negativity and despair

- Disappointment

- Shame

- Feelings of unworthiness

- Feelings of being cursed

- Blaming ourselves for past actions

- Resenting people who have caused us pain

Many shamanic cultures believe that we agree to incarnate in this lifetime in order to work out old karma and challenging issues. These are called sacred contracts. Some people might use the word "destiny." If fulfilling these contracts has lowered your quality of life, created abusive relationships, or created other unhealthy patterns, you can perform a ceremony to release or modify a contract that is no longer serving you. These contracts contain essential soul lessons, and they are not always easy to learn. Even a successful ceremony might not break a contract completely, but it can create gentler life situations to give you the same lesson. I have witnessed many miraculous changes from ceremonies with the intention to lighten or modify a soul contract.

Carrying old wounds is an emotional and physical burden. Dissolving anchors to a past that no longer serves you can allow you to create the life you dream of for yourself and the Earth.

Before performing any releasing ceremony, remember to call in the help of your compassionate spirits, ancestors, and the ancestors of the land who always "have your back."

When You Feel Cursed

In the practice of shamanism, it is understood that thoughts are things. As I explained in the introduction, there is a difference between expressing energy and sending energy. When we do not recognize and honor the unseen impact of the energy of our thoughts, we are often unaware that we are sending anger to another or into the collective. The effect of this negative energy is that many people today feel like they have been cursed. Others might feel cursed if they believe they are carrying a generational curse from their ancestral line.

We are all one. Whatever energy we send to another, we also send to ourselves and loved ones. To protect ourselves, our loved ones, and all of life from toxic energies, we must use discipline to express our feelings and then transform the energy. The ceremonies I share in this chapter are about releasing our own negative energy as well as energy we might have received from others. This important healing ceremonial work will free you to live out your destiny.

Review of Your Preparation

To prepare for your ceremony, review "Setting Your Intention" in chapter 4 and decide whether you wish to work alone or in a group.

Sacred healing can happen when you hold your attention, intention, and focus on what needs to be healed. Setting an intention alone has the power to heal. Adding action to intention by performing a releasing ceremony greatly magnifies that power.

If you practice shamanic journeying, you can consult with your helping spirits. The advantage of working through the intermediary helping spirits is that they can help you identify when you are framing an intention that might not be in your best interest or that might be simply reinforcing old childhood patterns. For example, your helping spirits will be honest with you and encourage you to delve into issues around forgiveness that you might not want to look at. The helping spirits are your buddies and want to see you succeed.

If you don't have a journeying practice, there are many ways to tap into your deep intuitive wisdom to discover what you need to release.

Meditate, pray, journal, draw, or reflect as you sit or walk in nature, or just sit quietly with a cup of tea. Some people tap into their deeper wisdom through listening to music and dancing. Use whatever practice works for you to help you learn what you need to release in order to find inner freedom and move forward to a more creative and healthier phase of life.

There is something special and supportive in performing healing ceremonies with friends or family. In performing releasing ceremonies, I am so touched as I drum and rattle and join the group in cheering people on as they release a pain, wound, or blocking belief. The level of support is so loving. For many people, including myself, being witnessed performing a ceremony for releasing a past wound or belief is transformative and healing in itself. If you feel ready, invite members in your local community to create a bonfire where each person burns an effigy or paper that symbolizes a personal hurt.

Yet there are also times when I like to be alone as I light a fire in my fireplace to release a prayer stick that represents my pain or a piece of paper with words written to the Creator or to those I need to forgive. Or I write beliefs that need to be released on paper and burn it with herbs or wood chips in a sacred bowl while I have candles and incense burning. I like to do the preparation alone, work with the fire, chant while my effigy burns, and then sit for hours while communicating with my helping spirits and the fire itself. The feeling that comes from hearing the vibration of my chanting with the burning flames is sacred.

I use dissolving paper for many of my personal releasing ceremonies. Sitting by my altar with a candle lit and my bowl of warm water in front of me, I write on a piece of dissolving paper a belief, hurt, or issue I am ready to release. I chant as I watch it dissolve fully. Then I ceremonially take the bowl outside and feed it to the earth in gratitude for taking my pain and composting it into love and light that will support new life to grow within me and in nature. Sometimes I rattle and sing as the words flow through me while addressing the power of the universe, the spirit of Santa Fe, and the helping ancestors of the land.

I have collected stories from people who build very small altars with stones in parks near their homes. They go to these altars in the morning to perform their daily ceremony of singing their prayers for peace, for healing, and for the world. During this time, they release any issues that prevent a feeling of hope for a good day. It is a lovely way to start the day.

Over time you will learn to trust your feelings about whether you wish privacy in performing your ceremony or if you want a supportive community witnessing and celebrating your transformational work.

Always remember to imagine the energy you are releasing being transformed into an energy of love and light that nurtures the elements and the collective at large.

FIRE CEREMONIES FOR RELEASING

Fire ceremonies are wonderful to perform, and they create an ecstatic state for participants. The nature of fire is energetic and transformative. It is easy to feel the power of the fire enlivening us. Fire ceremonies have been used and are still used in shamanic cultures worldwide. In many shamanic cultures, fire ceremonies go on all night, and the celebration of the work performed continues with watching the rising sun and sharing food together.

In performing a fire ceremony with a group, review the directions in "Gathering Your Materials" in chapter 2. Invite participants to create an effigy or power object from items in nature. Advise everyone to do spiritual work to draw out the energy they wish to put in the fire and place it into the effigy or power object so that it embodies the issue being released.

Join with others to decorate the space. Whether the fire ceremony is inside or outside, you want to have volunteers who create sacred space, greet each person to spiritually cleanse them, and welcome them into the circle. One or more people can perform an invocation. You can take turns greeting the compassionate spirits.

Although I ask people to stand during the ceremony, I have chairs for those who are not able to stand for a long time. I ask the fire keepers to clean and rake the area of objects on the ground that people can trip on. If the moon is dark, I ask people to bring flashlights to place in the circle around the fire so that people can see their paths.

Everyone can drum and rattle, supporting the person performing the releasing work as they place their power object or effigy in the fire. I bring some cedar or sacred herbs, so each person can give it as an offering to the fire. I instruct participants not to leave the ceremony (unless there is an emergency) until the ceremony is completed. To leave in the middle of a ceremony would be disrespectful to the group and the helping spirits.

Instead of having participants go in a specific order, let people choose when it feels right to step up to the fire to release their effigy. I ask people to work one by one instead of having multiple people releasing at the same time. When too many people go to the fire simultaneously, an uncontained energy is created, and there is not as much power in the ceremony.

I invite people to dance the energy of what they are releasing. They can also dance as they finish their work in celebration and as they step back into the circle. Many people do not feel comfortable dancing in front of a group or are physically unable to do so. I let people know they can simply walk up to the fire and place in what they need to release. Some people need an escort to help them get to the fire if they can't do it on their own. The group cheers on each person as they release their blocking belief into the fire.

Keep people moving along with their releasing work. I have attended fire ceremonies where there was a space of 15 minutes before the next person stepped up to the fire to place in their talisman. There is no way for people to stay focused when a ceremony is so slow and somber. Although this ceremony involves the releasing of pain, it is a joyful act of healing.

Always practice basic safety when using fire. Fire keepers create sacred space, build the fire, welcome the group, keep feeding wood to the fire, and deal with any stray embers. Their final role after the ceremony has ended is to make sure the fire is entirely out.

THE BOOK OF CEREMONY

I end ceremonies with people dancing and singing around the fire, watching as it burns our effigies. Once the spirits, fire keepers, and participants have been thanked, and it is stated that the work is done, some people wish to stay and continue singing or praying, while those ready to leave can do so.

Working with Water

There are times when it is not appropriate to work with fire. The energy generated with working with water is feminine in nature. There is a different quality of the ceremony when working with placing paper in water.

There are more places on the planet experiencing drought where fire danger is high. Working with dissolving paper and water is a safe, magical practice for adults and children.

You can set up bowls of warm water and decorate your space. Greet the helping spirits and divine forces in your preparation work. You can play music in the background, or people can drum or rattle. Each participant can share the story of what they are releasing into the water. It creates deep bonding for any group to hear and witness the pain being released. I find it is more powerful when participants share their story after they've put their paper in the water. This allows the power to build in the body instead of being discharged too early.

Once the ceremony is closed and the work is done, the group can bring the bowls of water out to the land together, feeding the earth with love.

PATRICIA'S HEALING CEREMONY

This is an example of a ceremony that combines releasing wounds and asking for positive dreams to be blessed.

Patricia was dealing with a health challenge. She decided to create a ceremony in which her friends could support her. She asked friends to drum and rattle as she worked. She placed slips of prepared dissolving paper in the water and then spoke of each fear or issue she was releasing.

The ceremony soon took off on its own because Patricia's friends also wanted to release some of their burdens and challenges. One by one, each friend in the circle wrote or drew images on the dissolving paper, placed the paper in the water, and then shared a brief story of a sabotaging belief, someone who had to be forgiven, or an old haunting trauma. The group drummed, rattled, and chanted in support.

Once everyone had a chance to dissolve an issue, they repeated the process around the circle until each person felt they had emptied their list of things that were holding them back or contributing to challenging emotional or physical issues.

Next, it was time to fill the space inside each person with something positive. First, they emptied the bowls of water holding their pain and suffering onto the earth outside while perceiving the water feeding the earth with light and love. With fresh water, they continued the ceremony, with each person writing a blessing on paper and then stating it aloud as they placed it in the water. With each blessing, the group stopped and took a deep breath while imagining the vibration of the blessing filling them up with good health, joy, and peaceful thoughts. Finally, they emptied the bowls again onto the earth.

Each person felt energized, and no one wanted the ceremony to end. The group celebrated by drumming, rattling, and dancing. The long evening ended with songs. Patricia thanked the helping spirits and declared that the work was done as everyone cheered.

Some of the group members noticed they were feeling a bit ungrounded, so Donna, one of the participants, led a beautiful grounding meditation so that everyone left filled with good, positive energy and with deep roots connecting them to the earth.

Use the creative talents of the group you are working with to create a rich, fresh, and unique ceremony. There are so many ways to bring unlimited power into working with water. Effigies that won't pollute water can be made and given to a river, lake, or ocean.

Some of my students draw mandalas on the sand by the ocean. These mandalas are created with symbols representing what needs to be released or blessed. The tide washes the images and symbols away and takes the light-filled energies into the sea to be transformed or blessed. This ceremony is spectacular as it also reminds us that everything in life is impermanent. Imagine performing such a ceremony, chanting, and gazing at the beauty of the full moon radiating shimmering light on the sea, adding exponential energy to your ceremony.

Use your imagination and allow your heart and intention to be your guide.

Releasing into the Earth or Water

You can use your breath to blow your hurt or old beliefs into objects you find in nature. Stones can be used in a burial ceremony. Enter into a meditative state and ask the stone for permission to use it in ceremony, as shamans have done for thousands of years.

Instead of burying it, you can perform a releasing ceremony placing a stone or other natural object into the sea, a lake, a river, or even a waterfall. The beach mandala ceremony described above acts as an exquisite way to bury old hurts while calling in the best that life has to offer.

Wind Is an Ally

Some people love to work with fire. Others are drawn to working with earth, water, or air. There are many people who have a deep relationship with the wind. I know people who love to stand in strong winds to be cleansed of their hurts and old beliefs. Wind is a naturally cleansing force and a powerful ally to many. Remarkable wind stories have been shared cross-culturally since the beginning of time. Wind is my ally, and I depend on it for my most important guidance.

SAM'S RELEASING CEREMONY FOR CHILDREN

Sam taught second grade. One day he brought in bottles of bubbles for the class. Sam asked all the children to think about something bothering them and then led them outside. The sun was shining, and the air was very still. As each child started to release their hurts by blowing bubbles, the wind picked up, carrying the bubbles quickly away. They were instructed to see the energy sent into the air as love and light. The children were energized, and they giggled throughout the entire ceremony. Sam taught songs about the elements and how they can heal us and how they bring us all we need to survive. The children loved singing and would spontaneously break into dance from time to time.

Sam received great feedback from some of the children's parents when their children arrived home laughing, happy, centered, and at peace.

PRAYER TREES

Creating Prayer Trees is a wonderful way to work alone, with your family, with coworkers, or in your community.

I became fascinated with Prayer Trees after learning about the practice in Central Asia. Typically, a juniper tree is chosen by a shaman. The shaman and the community engage in days of invocations and leave offerings to the tree. They tie prayer ribbons loosely on the branches, so the wind and the tree will share the prayers with the creative forces of the universe.

In many cultures, trees are seen as sacred beings bridging Heaven and Earth. Photos of Prayer Trees in Central Asia show branches almost touching the ground due to the weight of all the colorful ribbons tied on. Prayer Trees also represent the World Tree, which in shamanism connects the Lower World, the Middle World, and the Upper World. There are Prayer, Blessing, and Wishing Trees around the world that have existed for generations.

Imagine the power of creating a Prayer Tree for your family, in your community, or even in the workplace, where everyone comes together to support each other's healing and wishes with each ribbon or piece of yarn attached to the tree.

First, find a tree in nature that is willing to carry your prayers to the divine forces. Perform your invocation and leave offerings alone or with a group. Once the Prayer Tree has been honored, you can invite people to tie colored ribbons or pieces of yarn that hold their healing prayer or wish onto a branch of the tree. As you can imagine, children love working with Prayer Trees.

It is important to honor the tree with offerings of water, flowers, sacred herbs, or whatever you feel is a good offering to leave. Please tie the ribbon or yarn loosely on the branch so as not to choke it, for the branches will continue to grow over time.

ANN'S MIRACULOUS STORY

I received a wonderful email from Ann, who had miraculous results working with a Prayer Tree. I wrote about creating Prayer Trees in my books *Walking in Light* and *Speaking with Nature* (coauthored with Llyn Roberts).

Ann created a Prayer Tree to help her cousin who had developed painful and life-threatening sacral spine wounds as a result of being wheelchair-bound. Ann empowered many pieces of yarn with focused intention to heal the wounds and tied each one on her tree.

In less than two weeks, her cousin's wounds first diminished in size, then completely vanished. His visiting nurse was amazed, as no conventional treatment had worked in the six months of trying to heal the wounds.

In the world of medicine, this rapid wound closure would be considered "impossible."

The healing seemed to extend beyond Ann's cousin's physical disability. It affected his attitude. He no longer thinks of himself as a victim of his disability and has now started his own practice of praying on behalf of friends and family.

As you can imagine, Ann and her cousin are so grateful!

KYLE CREATES A PUBLIC PRAYER TREE

Kyle wandered in a park and found a tree that was honored to be a Prayer Tree. Some of his friends joined him in invoking the intention, asking the tree to carry prayers up to the creative forces of the universe. They inaugurated the tree with offerings and tied their own strips of fabric imbued with prayers onto branches of the Prayer Tree.

Kyle left fabric strips near the tree for others to use. He and his friends spread the word about the tree and how to tie on the prayer strips. Over time, Kyle found he had to keep replenishing the fabric strips as the ceremony caught on in his community, and the tree became filled with prayers.

I love having a Prayer Tree outside my house where I can leave healing prayers for myself, my family, friends, and other loved ones. It is a place where I can leave prayers for forgiveness and release old hurts, blocking beliefs, despair, feelings of hopelessness, and issues around my physical health, to be entrusted to the power of the universe. I also tie on prayers to bless others, all of life, and the Earth.

I use my spinning wheel to spin fiber into yarn holding the intention of my prayer. I continue to leave beads, herbs, corn meal, water, and other gifts for the tree. I rattle and let songs flow through me as I pray for myself and others. Singing and rattling is also how I share my gratitude for answered prayers.

An incredible force of healing and love is generated in communities where residents can gather together to create a Prayer Tree and tie on prayers and blessings for themselves, each other, and the planet.

9

Working in the
Unseen Realms

Most of the ceremonies I've shared so far have been rooted in the physical world. While this is a powerful way to work, it is, as I've mentioned, not the only choice. Since the true magic of ceremony occurs on the level of spirit, working in the unseen realms can be just as effective as working in a physical space. A group of friends or family who cannot meet in the physical world can still perform a ceremony in the unseen realms with positive results.

Get familiar with the technology you want to use for a virtual ceremony. You might want one person to drum, but drumming over the phone or the internet may sound distorted. In such cases, a prerecorded track might be clearer, and people can sing or speak over the track. Participants can envision themselves drumming and rattling while in a guided meditation, or they can physically drum, rattle, sing, and dance during the ceremonial work in the unseen realms.

If you lead a virtual ceremony, use the "Guided Meditation to Create an Altar in the Unseen Realms" in chapter 5 to take people to your altar in the nonordinary realms. Use the description of opening the veils between the worlds as each person visualizes stepping out their front door. Or create your own guided journey or meditation to bring your group to the altar room or ceremonial space in the unseen world.

Describe the path and the landscape in detail. Focus on what people will see, smell, hear, feel, and taste. This will help each person be fully present as they walk the path. They will engage as if they are actually walking through a beautiful place in nature instead of watching themselves walking on the path as if it were a movie.

I will now share a powerful ceremony to release an old hurt. I've used this cauldron of light practice in my groups as a ceremony of forgiveness. The act of forgiveness dissolves unhealthy energetic bonds that keep us trapped in unhealthy relationships. The cauldron of light works in the unseen realms much in the way a fire ceremony does in the physical world.

ROBERT'S CAULDRON OF LIGHT

Robert had a terminal illness and wanted to feel complete before he died. He loved working with the cauldron of light to practice forgiveness.

Before each ceremony, Robert called his helping spirits into his virtual altar room. In this space, he envisioned a cauldron filled with brilliant, cleansing light. His guardian spirit met him with love and brushed away any energies that would contaminate the sacred field of the altar space. This was a safe and holy place for Robert to work.

Robert took many journeys to forgive himself for actions in his past. Each time, he envisioned placing words or drawings into the cauldron of light. Then he always moved to journeying on the people in his life that he needed to forgive. Robert understood that each shamanic journey is a ceremony. As so often happens in journeys, Robert's helping spirits gave him valuable and sometimes unexpected information about what he needed to transform, helping him uncover unconscious feelings of shame, blame, and regret.

Robert worked to forgive as many people as he needed to forgive in order to experience a state of peace, so he could die without carrying grudges into another lifetime.

The cauldron of light works as a shared practice with others. Your group might envision walking through the veil between the seen and unseen realms into a beautiful garden where there is a great cauldron of light. Once there, you perform your ceremony in the nonordinary realms to release and transform negative states of consciousness.

PERFORMING FIRE CEREMONIES IN THE NONORDINARY REALMS

I lead groups in performing a releasing ceremony in the virtual realms.

After preparing, I lead the group past the altar room to a meadow where they see a distant bonfire. Guardian spirits cleanse each person before they enter the circle. I tell the group there are bowls filled with effigy objects for the fire, such as prayer sticks with colored yarn wrapped around them or medicine bundles filled with herbs. Each person picks the object that calls to them.

After the invocation, we gaze upon the beauty of the night sky. We listen to the fire crackling, smell the smoke, and look into the beauty of the circle. The drumming and rattling begins. Participants place their effigy objects imbued with the pain they are releasing into the fire as the drumming, rattling, chanting, and dancing continues. With virtual ceremonies, including physical activity like singing and drumming helps people engage more deeply.

We feed sacred herbs into the fire in gratitude for taking our pain and transforming it to loving and light-filled energies that feed the collective. I end by guiding people back to the room they are journeying or meditating in and lead a short grounding exercise, asking people to connect deeply with the earth.

VIVIAN AND THE SACRED CAVE

Vivian's group wanted to work in a virtual territory that felt more earthy than an enclosed altar room. She designed a guided meditation to lead people to a sacred cave in the unseen realms. Vivian and her group drummed and rattled as they made the journey to this place, strongly imagining each sense coming alive with their surroundings.

A great fire burned in the middle of this dark cave. Vivian and her group danced and sang around the fire. Everyone released the power object, letters, or drawings they had made into the transformative power of fire.

CREATING A VIRTUAL PRAYER TREE

A Prayer Tree is a living altar to work at, a place to tie on prayers for any purpose while sitting in silence, absorbing the power and wisdom of the tree. It is not always possible to find a tree in nature that is appropriate to work with, especially if you live in an urban area, but you can create a virtual Prayer Tree no matter where you are. Although you can work with a virtual Prayer Tree alone, it is a special experience to be able to bring together friends, loved ones, coworkers, or students to tie their prayers onto a tree existing in the unseen realms. Imagine people from around the world working together with one beautiful Prayer Tree.

I have led guided meditations and journeys to take groups of people from all over the world to a beautiful Prayer Tree in the unseen realms to tie on prayers on behalf of ourselves, others, all of life, and the Earth. After our preparation work, I lead the group past the virtual altar room to a giant old-growth tree whose width is enormous and whose branches reach gracefully to the sky.

We invoke the helping spirits and then chant or speak words of thanks to the tree for taking our prayers for healing, blessings, and peace to the creative forces of the universe, which will work with us in partnership to make our prayers so.

The guardian spirits cleanse each person. We gather around, taking in the beauty and wonder of the tree and surrounding nature.

I tell the group that there are bowls with prayer ribbons. We each tie prayers very loosely on the branches and then return to the circle. The group's singing, drumming, and rattling supports each person. Participants leave gifts of flowers or something else from nature that represents beauty, love, and gratitude as an offering for the tree and the helping spirits.

After closing the ceremony, I lead participants back home through the veils of the unseen into the physical.

AUDREY'S PRAYER TREE

Audrey decided to create a Prayer Tree for a group of family members who live throughout Australia. A beloved relative was having severe health issues, and she asked her family to join her in the adventure of working in meditation with a Prayer Tree.

Audrey used an online program to have everyone on video while she drummed and rattled as she led the ceremony. She guided everyone to walk through a rainforest, with vines brushing each person as they walked. The vines cleansed everyone by brushing away their ordinary concerns and burdens. The vines formed an arbor, leading them deeper into nonordinary reality realms.

Audrey described everything in detail, asking each person to feel the soft, rich soil beneath their feet and feel the mist and humidity of the rainforest acting as a container for their collective field of energy. She described the sun shining through the trees, so everyone could soak in the warmth, smell the fragrances, and even taste the salt in the air.

They came to a magnificent and exquisite tree in a clearing. Audrey asked everyone to walk to the tree and stand in silence while appreciating the power of the tree and their love for each other. They focused on their intention for healing their relative while holding loving hands.

Audrey chanted as she cleansed them with incense, asking everyone to put aside their fears and thoughts to focus on the prayers they wanted to tie on the tree. The family took prayer ribbons from the offering bowls and tied on prayers for their ailing loved one. They also took the opportunity to tie on prayer ribbons for world peace. They left petals of their favorite flowers as offerings—rose, dandelion, and sunflower—and then were guided back home.

This ceremony touched Audrey's family as they let go of their conflicts and joined together for the healing of a loved one. Their hearts expanded, and they bonded deeply in ways that continued over time. Each continued to visit the Prayer Tree through meditation. They experienced peace as they sat with the Prayer Tree and reflected on their own lives and the lives of loved ones. They continued to leave ribbons of prayers for healing. Their beloved family member who was ill made a great deal of process in her healing through the love and prayers offered to her. They were so grateful to this massive tree being who helped focus their prayers.

Audrey was touched to watch four generations of family come together to perform a ceremony. This alone was an enormous act of healing.

PUTTING YOUR TRUST IN YOUR HELPING SPIRIT OR DIVINE ALLY

Sometimes, the most powerful ceremonial work you can do is to place your trust completely in a helping spirit, divine ally, or the power of the universe.

To start, do your preparation work as you would for any ceremony. Use drumming, spiritually expansive music, or any technique that helps you step out of ordinary life into sacred space. In the unseen realms, ask to meet with your helping spirit.

Once you are with your compassionate spirit, state your intention of what needs to be released or healed. Ask your helping spirit or divine being to unwind this pain or trauma, something that needs to be forgiven, or another issue. Your helping spirit will unwind threads out of the core of your being into a shimmering ball of light that they will release to an element to be transformed.

This is a powerful healing ceremonial experience. It is also an intimate time with your helping spirit or divine force as you release to them a pain, belief, trauma, something that needs forgiving, or an old sacred contract that needs to be broken. It is a true act of surrender and a beautiful way to heal.

DELORES RELEASES HER BINDS

Delores came to see me as a client. She had been in psychotherapy for years, attended classes on meditation, and focused on exercise and eating a healthy diet. Despite her best efforts, her life felt off track. She found herself in abusive relationships, a dead-end job, dealing with financial problems, and feeling like she was not in the flow of life.

I performed healing work with Delores and taught her how to perform a healing ceremony in the nonordinary realms. Using all the elements of ceremony, Delores met the divine and compassionate spirit Mother Mary. Through direct telepathic contact, Mother Mary told Delores about a sacred contract she had made during a past life, when she had agreed to sacrifice her needs. In this past life, she was a bit selfish and was not a compassionate wife or mother.

Mother Mary compassionately held Delores and assured her that this contract was fulfilled but that she was stuck repeating old patterns from her past. The cycle of sacrificing joy for misery needed to be broken for Delores to grow. Mother Mary asked Delores if she was ready to let go of this old binding contract. Delores was thrilled to work with a divine figure that she had so much love and trust for.

Mother Mary reached into Delores's solar plexus and started unwinding what looked like shimmering blue yarn. Then Mother Mary blew on the yarn, which transformed into little roses that rained down on Delores, signifying that the contract was broken and fulfilled and that it was now time to embrace the beauty of life.

Then, Mother Mary filled Delores with light, so she was whole.

TIGER DISMEMBERS MARTIN'S CONTRACT

Martin felt like he was under a curse. In ceremony, he met his helping spirit, Tiger, who told Martin about an old contract that now needed to be let go of. Tiger used a dismemberment ceremony—a powerful and ancient practice that allows a helping spirit or ally dissolve energetic blockages. Martin felt no fear or pain as Tiger's paws reached into his heart, pulled out a contract, and tore it apart.

Martin felt immediately lighter after Tiger dismembered and devoured the contract, which had bound up his joy and ability to create a healthy life.

Martin's Tiger then filled him with light. He also performed a general healing on him to make sure Martin felt whole and filled with love and power.

Use any ceremony I've described or one you design on your own to let go of life's disappointments. I love the unwinding ceremony, dismemberment, and cauldron of light when I work with helping spirits or divine forces to release disappointments. I suggest this work to those who are disappointed when their ceremonial work did not lead immediately to their desired outcome.

Part Four

LIFE AS A CEREMONY

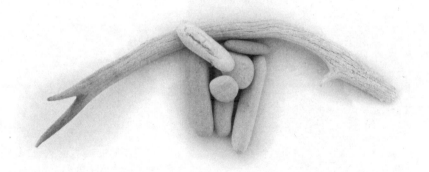

10

BLESSING AND HEALING
CEREMONIES FOR PEOPLE

Whater we engage in personal healing work, we feel more whole, present in our lives, and filled with a greater sense of who we are.

Healing and blessing work helps us create a world that reflects our inner landscape. We want to live in houses filled with positive energy, create strong and healthy relationships, connect in profound ways to the cycles of nature, honor our land or the city we live in, and work on creating the life we wish to live, as well as supporting a good dream for the planet.

Blessing ceremonies can be used to:

- Call in your life's dream or work

- Restore the soul (life force and loving energies) to your house, your land, an office, or your community

- Help you transition to a new home, job, part of the world, project, or a new phase of life

- Support a new garden or a community garden

- Ask for a positive outcome for someone having surgery, going to war, or facing a life change

- Call in protection when driving, flying, presenting at a business meeting, or doing anything in a collective energetic space that feels toxic

- Honor birthdays, anniversaries, and holidays

- Honor the new moon, full moon, equinox, and solstice

- Express your gratitude and honor for the land where you live, the nature beings where you live, the elements, and your life

- Bring healing spiritual light to help loved ones, clients, and all of life

- Bless anything or anyone else you want to add to this list

It's very powerful to combine the releasing ceremonies I describe in part 3 with ceremonies for healing and blessing. In such cases, you would finish the releasing and then clear the space by burning sacred herbs or by singing and dancing. State an invocation that now that old wounds, blocking, and self-sabotaging beliefs have been released, you will continue to manifest your wishes and desires for yourself, the web of life, and the Earth.

In some circumstances you might want to reverse these ceremonies to first call in your blessing and then perform a ceremony releasing blocking beliefs preventing you from receiving your desired outcome. For example, you might need to release feeling unworthy to manifest the blessing you requested.

There are no rules about what order to follow when you perform a releasing ceremony and blessing ceremony. Follow your own inner flow.

Envisioning a Good Life

While performing your releasing ceremonies, envision what you want to manifest in your life. It is good to do these processes together—letting go and also focusing on what you have to look forward to in receiving the goodness of life.

In the practice of shamanism, life is seen as a dream. What you daydream about while going to work, taking walks, eating, and so on, also reflects and helps create the life you are now living and how you are contributing to the events we're witnessing on the planet.

If throughout the day you daydream about how you hate your life, your job, political issues, and so on, you end up feeding the seeds you are planting in your inner garden. Your daydreams will germinate and grow into strong plants. You need to decide on how you truly want to design the garden of your inner landscape.

A powerful shamanic teaching is that if you want to change your life, you have to change your daydreams. Yes, so many of us are afraid of failure. But remember, performing ceremonies is not about creating an "immediate win." We perform ceremonies to plant seeds in our inner world that through time, cultivation, and nurturing grow plants of great beauty whose qualities infuse our lives and the world.

When you're embarking on any adventure, such as starting a relationship, moving to a new home or city, finding meaningful work, or even returning to school to learn new skills, begin with a strong, positive vision. Focus on what you look forward to in the present and future.

Another metaphor that shamans like to use is that our daydreams weave into the tapestry of life we are creating. A classic shamanic teaching is that our destiny is to be dreamers and to focus on a good dream for all of life.

Before performing a ceremony to bring in the best that life has to offer, there is some preparation work to do to engage your imagination. In this way, your spirit continues to commune with the divine and creative forces of the universe.

Many people underestimate "imagination" as it relates to shamanism. They think it means we are just making up artificial experiences. But we make up everything that occurs in our outer world. Without imagination, we would not engage the senses needed to journey or perform guided meditations. Everything we experience in our inner and outer world is what we are imagining. Imagination creates our reality.

Reflect on what you want to manifest in your life—whether this is for your own health and joy, for your loved ones, for your community, or for the Earth.

Once you have the intention of your life's dream, start to imagine yourself already living the life you wish for. Focus on each sensory detail. Move away from a two-dimensional process of watching your desired life as if it were a movie. Make your dream three-dimensional and fully step into the life you desire and the world you wish to live in. Imagine it so completely that you bring your dream to life.

For example, when desiring healthy relationships with friends, imagine their smiling and loving faces, their features, and their clothes. Are these new friends, or are you deepening your current relationships? Imagine your conversations. Touch one of your friend's hands in a supportive and loving way. Notice your surroundings. Are you in a restaurant together? What does the restaurant look like? How is it decorated? Imagine yourself eating together. What are you eating, and what does the food taste like? What is the weather like outside?

Smell the fragrances of the air. Imagine yourself laughing or crying during touching times. After you leave the restaurant and continue visiting with your friends, imagine walking through a charming landscape. Feel the texture of the earth, the gentle wind, and the objects in your environment.

Continue engaging your senses to bring yourself fully into the life situation you are dreaming about. We are dreaming all the time when we use our imagination.

Expand your dreaming work to include engaging in loving and healthy scenes with your family, feeling hopeful, and living in a pristine environment and world that embraces love, peace, honor, and respect for all of life.

Step fully into the dream you are imagining as if it has already been created and you are living the life you wish. Live that life fully in your imagination. See out of your eyes as you live your new life. Listen to the sounds. Feel your surroundings and the joy of your desired and healthy life. Engage fully by experiencing yourself eating and drinking, by touching your environment with your hands, and by smelling the fragrances as you move around in your newly manifested world.

Here's an example of another way to work with daydreaming before performing a blessing ceremony. When I feel I have fallen out of the flow of life, I imagine myself paddling a canoe down a spectacular river, flowing gracefully as the river twists and turns, going over turbulent waters, and then paddling through the smooth waters that come. First, I feel the flow of life in my body before designing a blessing ceremony to ask that my life return to a natural flow.

Once you have established a dreaming practice on a regular basis, there are a wealth of ceremonies you can use for asking for your wishes and your dreams to be blessed.

Fire Ceremonies for Blessing Your Greatest Dreams

In my trainings, when we work together to manifest our dreams, we perform a fire ceremony to ask that our wishes be blessed and supported. We often begin by doing the work I described earlier for releasing old wounds into a fire before we begin asking for blessings.

While crafting a talisman, effigy, or power object, stay focused on imagining your desire.

In building the fire, let it know how it can work in partnership with you or your group. In other ceremonies, we have invoked fire's power to transmute and transform. Here, we are asking the smoke to take your prayers up to the universe. It is important to build the fire with the intention you are asking for. Ask the fire to take your prayers and wishes up to the forces of the universe to make them manifest. In this way, your creative energy synchronizes with the divine creative forces.

When deciding to combine both a releasing and blessing fire ceremony, let the fire know that you will be doing both. Know that the spirit of the fire is listening and working with you. Each ceremony will deepen your relationship with the ally of fire.

Now I'll share an adaptation of this fire ceremony for blessing our dreams. When we tap into the principle of oneness, we realize that we all have a collective dream. Whatever I am dreaming for is part of your dream too.

In this version, first the fire keepers place a blanket in a clearing where the group will gather around the fire. Each person is spiritually cleansed and greeted into the circle. Everyone places their talismans on the blanket. After the invocation and the drumming, rattling, and chanting begins, each person picks up someone else's talisman to place in the fire.

It is amazing to watch the power and joy as a person asks for the blessing of someone else's dream to come to pass. I love how the circle's energy becomes so supportive as everyone shares their full attention and energy as they watch their dream go into the fire.

We end by dancing and praying for the children of all species who cannot express for themselves their dream for a life filled with love, a good place to live, enough food and water, and to be honored and respected. I thank the spirits and close the ceremony.

JAKE'S CEREMONY TO HELP HIS COMMUNITY

Jake's hometown suffered devastating tornadoes, and many residents were in despair after losing their homes as well as suffering emotionally, physically, and financially. It felt like the collective of the community had lost its soul. Recalling a fire ceremony we'd done, Jake spoke to me about wanting to bring this ceremony back home to bless his community.

Jake was nervous because he knew his community would not embrace shamanic practice. I shared with him how I had led this same ceremony in the pilot research study for people who had suffered a heart attack. I had welcomed everyone into the circle with sweet-sounding bells and handed out various shamanic instruments. Jake adapted this practice by making rattles using glass bottles with popcorn kernels inside.

Since creating talismans or effigies seemed like too much of a stretch, Jake provided pens and paper, and each person wrote their wishes on a piece of paper. Volunteers built the fire. The children in the community decorated the space. The community supported each person as they placed their papers into the fire to be blessed. The children laughed for the first time in weeks as they got their turn to feed the fire with their wishes. The group sang inspirational songs before and after the ceremony.

Sometime later, Jake sent me a thank-you note. Not everyone in the community chose to show up for the ceremony, but most did. They had a beautiful evening gathering to dream together and reestablish a state of hope. The light in people's eyes returned.

They ended the ceremony talking about how they could be a greater support to each other in rebuilding their homes and community. Jake said that the deep and binding healing that occurred in his community was beyond his wildest dream.

ADAPTATIONS OF BLESSING CEREMONIES

The Prayer Tree ceremony can easily be used for blessing and healing. A group, family, community, or workplace can create a Prayer Tree together, either with a physical tree or as a virtual ceremony. Over time, people can continue to tie their prayer ribbons or yarn on the branches of the tree. Some people tie on prayer ribbons asking to be relieved of a pain or trauma, while some tie on wishes that they would like to see manifest. Tie on ribbons or yarn containing prayers for someone having surgery, going through a treatment for an illness, going off to war, or facing a life change. You can also ask for protection when traveling, presenting your ideas at a business meeting, or doing anything that might take you into an energetically toxic space.

Water ceremonies are also powerful for blessing and healing. Set a bowl of warm water on your altar and write your wishes on dissolving paper. Light a candle, play music, state your invocation, and place the paper in the water, continuing your prayers as it dissolves. Ceremonially release the water filled with loving energies into the earth, a body of water, or even into the wind. You can do this alone, in a group, or as a virtual ceremony.

I encourage you to create your own unique ceremonies and improvise on what I have shared in this book. I have found designs and structures for my ceremonies that feel good to me to perform personally and to lead in my groups. I find that every time I repeat a ceremony, it is like walking the same path again, where my footsteps create a deepening in my path. When repeating ceremonies, make sure they don't become habitual, where you feel there is no longer life to them. The energy and passion you put into your ceremonial work makes a difference in the power of the ceremony and the results.

STUART AND ANNE'S CEREMONY FOR CRISIS

Stuart and Anne, brilliant shamanic teachers, lived in an area devastated by fire. Everyone in the community had experienced some degree of loss, from losing a friend, losing a home, or being evacuated, to living without water or power, being displaced to a shelter, endless smoke, and the National Guard on the streets. People throughout the city were suffering from post-traumatic stress.

Stuart and Anne invited community members to take part in a blessing ceremony to ask for healing for the community and to bless people who needed to rebuild their lives. Adults and children of all ages were welcome at the ceremony. People of different races, sexual orientations, and gender identities showed up to help support each other.

They set up a table with food offerings of fruit, favorite treats, and crystal hearts. Everyone was given a chance to talk and share their feelings—not just with each other, but also to the spirit of Fire. People shared their sadness and fears and also what they were grateful for. After a devastating event, we often realize how much we still have to be grateful for in life.

Drumming, rattling, and singing all went on for quite a long time. Everyone was asked to imagine themselves sending good wishes into the food and crystals on the table. Each person was invited to eat the offerings energized with blessings and to take a crystal heart filled with blessing energy that they could hold and keep.

Blessing and Healing
Ceremonies for Places

As your proficiency with ceremony increases, you'll be able to perform longer ceremonial work that might stretch over days or weeks. Eventually, you'll integrate ceremony into each day, so you live in harmony with the sacred. This chapter will help you focus bringing ceremony into your everyday life.

While conducting research for my second book, *Welcome Home: Following Your Soul's Journey Home*, I found a reference in the ethnographic literature about shamans calling back the soul of crops. This led me to a new line of thinking, expanding my work from performing soul retrievals on people and other nature beings to returning the soul of the places where we live and work.

Performing soul retrievals for people and nature beings is beyond the scope of this book. These powerful healing ceremonies for people and other living beings who have suffered a trauma require serious and committed training in performing shamanic healing work. Yet I have found that the practice of performing soul retrievals for places is easier to learn and can have remarkable results.

The definition of soul is "essence" or "life force." Our homes have a soul, as does the land we live on, buildings, cities, and so on.

When we engage in deep spiritual work, we develop greater awareness of the energy around us. We can feel the difference between entering a house filled with sterile or toxic energy and walking into a home that is vibrant and alive. The same is true with places—including the land we live on, the offices we work in, the neighborhoods we live in, and our cities.

In shamanic cultures, homes and structures are built with attention to honoring all the materials used. Every stone is blessed. Trees are blessed before cutting them down for wood. Songs are sung while building to fill the home with good energy.

Today we tend to build as cheaply and quickly as possible without paying attention to the materials or honoring the essence of the home or building.

Sometimes homes, buildings, and the land where we live do not contain vital energy because they are not spiritually honored. Land can be traumatized through war or violence.

You can perform ceremonies to call back and honor the soul of a house, building, office, or land that has been traumatized or neglected. Ceremony can restore harmony, peace, and a sense of beauty and vitality. In this way, the places where you live and work reflect back the strength and beauty of your soul.

Singing back the soul of a home, land, or place is a classic shamanic way to work.

Blessing a Home

In the 1980s, I was traveling to and teaching at about forty weekend workshops per year. I was not in Santa Fe much, but friends invited me to stay in their guest house when I was home. I lived in a tiny room that had a desk, a chair, and a bed built into the wall.

I met with clients in this room, and we could just about fit. If they brought family or friends for support, we had to crowd on the floor together, which always ended up being a wonderful bonding experience.

I handwrote my first book, *Soul Retrieval: Mending the Fragmented Self*, on the desk in my room. I lived and worked in this room for about five years, and I felt it was immersed with powerful healing energy. I truly wanted to live in that tiny room forever.

When the family I lived with announced they were moving, I was traumatized. I could not imagine leaving my sacred space.

I moved into my partner's home, where he had built a new office for me to work in. Before moving, I journeyed for a ceremony that I could perform to help me energetically move from my precious sanctuary to my new office.

I was guided to rattle and chant. A song flowed through me effortlessly. While chanting, I imagined winding the positive energy of the room into my rattle. I continued chanting until I felt no more spiritual energy in the room. I took the rattle to my new office and chanted another song that flowed from my soul while shaking out all the collected healing energy in the rattle into my new office.

This ceremony worked for me. I felt like my new office was filled with the years of good healing energy I had generated in my former room. I continued my ceremony with building a new altar in my office, bringing in flowers and sacred objects that honored my new healing space.

The new owners of my friends' house were spiritual healers. They shared with me that they bought the house because of the energy in my office. When I met the husband at a social gathering, he asked me where the energy in my office went. I replied, "I took it with me." We talked together for a while and joked a lot about this. The couple who bought the house were well-known healers who knew it was their responsibility to fill the space with their own sacred energy.

DANIELA BLESSES HER APARTMENT

Daniela was excited about moving into her new apartment and desired to make it a living sanctuary. She invited over friends. She had visited a park beforehand and collected sacred objects from nature. Her friends brought gifts of rocks, crystals, and flowers. She performed her ceremony on the new moon, when the energy of new beginnings is strong.

Everyone drummed and rattled softly so as not to disturb the neighbors while Daniela called in the helping spirits of the apartment and the building. She welcomed and greeted the directions and honored her compassionate ancestors and the helping ancestors of the land.

Daniela burned sage and took her group around each room of the apartment to clear any stagnant energy. She burned lovely lavender incense to call in the sweetness of life. Each friend contributed a gift from nature. Daniela and her friends connected with a divine force, then blew blessings with their words and energy into a rock, crystal, or flower.

Together they found nooks and crannies around the apartment to place these inspirited objects from nature. Daniela placed some of the sacred objects on her new altar, reflecting this transition.

Once done, they celebrated with food and by sharing stories and blessings for Daniela as she began a new phase of her life. The ceremony ended with singing songs, and Daniela luxuriated alone, enjoying her new sanctuary.

BRYCE AND ROBIN'S NEW HOME BLESSING

Bryce and Robin bought a home for their family. Though their finances were tight, they managed to find a house at a low price that had been on the market for years. They felt lucky to buy a house in a good neighborhood with good schools nearby for their three kids. But they were not in love with the house. It had a dark energy, and did not feel cozy or warm.

Before moving in, they invited friends and family to come over. Everyone was delighted that Bryce and Robin had found a place they could afford, but everyone could also feel the strangely lifeless energy of the house.

Bryce and Robin were students of shamanism, and they used the tools they had learned about ceremony to bring back the soul of the house to transform it into a true home filled with love and sweet energies. They asked their friends and family to entertain the possibility that spiritual methods could transform the energy of the house. They explained the basics of performing a ceremony, the need to release their daily thoughts, open to the power of love, and greet divine forces who would work in partnership to create their desired outcome.

Everyone was game. The first idea presented by a friend was to use the elements of ceremony to repaint the house. With each brushstroke, friends and family members shared love for the house in their own way.

First, the energy of the house was cleared through smudging— burning sage to clear out the stale energies. The energy in the house was in no way malicious. It just lacked light and a warm, inviting feeling.

Bryce and Robin stated an appropriate intention for their diverse group. People sang as they painted. Bryce and Robin spoke to the spirit of the house and asked it to return, and some people breathed out the energy of love into the paint that was being used. They completed necessary repairs while sending love to the house.

Loved ones brought simple but colorful decorations before Bryce and Robin moved in their furniture. When they were done, the house exuded a glow that impressed them all. They felt so good there, and no one wanted to leave.

Love heals all living things—including our homes.

Calling Back the Soul of an Office

Office buildings today are not built with a consciousness of blessing the building materials, respect for the beauty of the building, or honor for the land and its ancestral spirits.

People who are sensitive to their surroundings pick up the lack of energy of their workplace and might not feel invigorated, at peace, harmonious, or supported by the lack of soul of a building or office.

Some businesses might embrace the idea of employees organizing a blessing ceremony to bring vital energy into a building. For other businesses, it might feel inappropriate to perform a ceremony with drums, rattles, and incense. In most cases, there are ways to create a low-key ceremony for calling back the soul of an office.

Remember, intention is key with a ceremony. An elaborate ceremony is not always needed. A very simple ceremony can let the spirit of a place know it is being honored while its soul is restored.

CHARLES CALLS BACK THE SOUL OF HIS OFFICE

Charles spent many years studying to be a psychotherapist. He had a strong personal practice of working through his emotional issues and was diligent about taking care of his health. He began working at an agency with teens at risk.

Though he loved his work and was gifted at it, Charles dreaded going to work each day. He felt unwell in his office environment. He could not put his finger on the problem, but he knew it felt soulless, and he had to fight to keep his energy bright enough to fully engage with his clients. He felt drained by the energy of the building.

Although his agency was open to alternative ways of working, Charles didn't think he could broach the topic of negative energy with coworkers. He could see the lack of life in his coworkers' eyes, but he was not ready to talk to them about calling back the soul of the office.

Charles performed a simple ceremony fueled by his intention. He brought in fresh flowers every day. When he placed the flowers on his desk and in different parts of the office, he offered a silent prayer while calling back the soul of his office. He breathed deeply and imagined speaking to the energy of the building. He expressed his love and respect for this place where teens could come and experience deep care and healing from the therapists, and he focused on making the office a warm and sacred space for this essential work.

Charles placed objects from nature on his desk, filling the objects with prayers, words, and blessing thoughts, such as, "May all our clients feel loved and supported."

These small acts of blessing flowers and objects from nature for the building changed Charles's perception of his office.

Before leaving the office for the day, he said a prayer, releasing out of opened windows any energy that was not filled with love, light, harmony, beauty, joy, honor, and respect. This was his way of clearing the space, making it ready for the work of the next day.

Charles turned this simple ceremony of clearing and bringing in flowers into a daily practice. In time, he felt that the energy truly reflected a bright vibration that would light up everyone who entered the office. Once he felt the change take hold, he switched from a daily practice to performing his ceremony whenever he felt it was needed, or during special times such as the new and full moon.

The air in the office was no longer stale. There was a sweet fragrance birthed by the new sacred and vital energy. Charles perceived that his coworkers looked brighter, more energetic, and more joyous. He felt that his ceremony was successful in retrieving the life force of the building.

BLESSINGS FOR LAND

Land can be traumatized, and the soul of the land can be lost. Sometimes the trauma of violence on land can create energies that need to be cleared. But unless you have a good, solid base of shamanic teachings you can call on, do not start clearing negative energy on land. Discarnate souls who died on the land can inhabit your body and create a possession or illness. You need to be well trained in the art of filling yourself with divine light or the power of your helping spirits. This is work where you would want to call in experienced shamanic healers.

I will share resources where you can find an international list of trained shamanic practitioners who can perform clearing ceremonies for the land either by visiting the land or working remotely through a virtual ceremony. In shamanism, we work outside of time and space, so remote healing typically works as well as traveling to the land physically.

Even if you aren't trained to clear the trauma of a place, you can certainly bless land. You might have had the experience of walking onto a piece of land and getting a physical sensation in your body that the land you are walking on is lifeless and soulless. You may notice the trees and plants do not look healthy, and the land is devoid of any birds or animal life. There is a sense that some energy is missing.

How can you tell if land has experienced soul loss? Sometimes we anthropomorphize—we see destruction caused by natural disaster, and our own sorrow leads us to think the land has suffered soul loss. This is not always the case. The land might be healed and regenerated by the climatic event that will birth new growth.

An experienced shamanic practitioner can perform a journey to a helping spirit to diagnose if the land has lost its soul or if it is simply going through a process of evolution. Even if you aren't trained in this practice, you can still bless the land through ceremony. If a soul retrieval is needed, the soul will return during the blessing ceremony. Your ceremony can be as simple as drumming, rattling, and singing or chanting as you tell the land how much you love, honor, and respect it and make a commitment to care for it. It could be as simple as creating sacred cairns around the property, bringing in a state of soulfulness.

Whatever your background or the belief system of your community, always begin your invocation with the one I shared in chapter 3: "This is a circle of strength. This is a circle of power. We have gathered together in love and light to support each other as we do our important work to heal ourselves, all in the web of life, and for the Earth. We join our hearts together in love. And only that which is of the light is welcomed into our circle." This simple invocation ensures any spiritual energies on the land that need healing do not impact the health of anyone present at the ceremony. If you don't specify, any spirits might come. They might be discarnate souls who need healing. Use discipline with your invocations, and you and your community can work safely and leave free of any unwelcome energies.

CATHY AND RICARDO'S LAND CLEARING

Cathy and Ricardo felt a sense of soullessness on a piece of land near their home. This touched their heart deeply. They felt a despair and lack of vitality in the land. They were acutely aware of the lack of animal and bird life that should be inhabiting the land. They performed a shamanic journey to their helping spirits to ask for a ceremony to retrieve the soul of their land.

Based on the guidance they received, they invited friends to perform a fire ceremony to call back the soul of the land. Due to drought conditions, they could not safely build an open fire, but they used a barbecue to control the flames and made sure the fire was fully out when done. Their friends brought their children, which added an element of joy.

Everyone showed up with a shamanic instrument to play. Cathy and Ricardo took turns greeting the helping spirits, the directions, the benevolent ancestors of the land, and the Hidden Folk—the devic realm, fairies, elves, forest guardians, and angels.

After the invocation, they drummed and danced until they felt filled with love, light, and the divine power of the universe. Feeling a shift in consciousness, each participant found a stick that they could empower with a blessing for the land. Each stick was placed in the fire with the intention of the fire bringing their prayers and blessings to the spirit of the land, calling its essence home. They sang to the land, spoke to it, and expressed their love.

Afterward, they lay on the ground, gazed at the beauty of the moon and the stars, and imagined the land vibrant and glowing. They felt an enormous change in the energy that was now embracing them as they honored the land. The children danced and talked about all the fairies and bright blue orbs of light that showed up during the ceremony.

Over time, Cathy and Ricardo saw changes in the land. They spotted deer and foxes sometimes. The trees became healthier, a variety of plant life started growing, and the land was blessed with the beauty of birdsong.

JANIS SINGS BACK THE SOUL OF HER LAND

Janis lived in a location where she felt a strong intuition that the land had lost its soul. She created a medicine wheel out of stones to create a symbol that represented an opening for the soul's return.

Janis gathered friends, and they walked around the medicine wheel, singing to the compassionate ancestors of the land while calling back the soul of the land. They rattled and sang to the birds, the insects, the animals, and the plants while asking them to return. They allowed their songs to be inspirited, letting them spontaneously emerge. They whistled throughout the ceremony to call back the soul of the land and other nature beings.

They left offerings of corn meal and sacred herbs. They sat around the medicine wheel feeling the wind sharing messages with them for the healing work they did for the land. The warmth of the sun felt so supportive. The elements worked with them in cooperation to make their work successful. They felt that connecting with the flow of their inner spirit created communication with the soul of the land. As their songs flowed, the song of the land started to flow and emerge too.

CALLING BACK THE SOUL OF A CITY OR COMMUNITY

When I teach my Five-Day Soul Retrieval Training, we spend an afternoon journeying on how to call back the soul of a home, office, business, land, city, or community. I have collected wonderful case studies since introducing this work in 1990.

Remember, time only exists in our dimension of reality. The beauty of shamanic journeying is that we can travel outside of time to meet our compassionate ancestors in the unseen realms. I discovered during my practice and teaching that we can also journey to the people in the future who will be the descendants of the Earth. We will be their ancestors. We can receive valuable guidance from the helping spirits from the past and future in the timeless, nonordinary realms.

I've taught students to journey to compassionate ancestral spirits or descendants to ask for ceremonies to return the soul of a place. I've found that the ancestors cannot always understand why a house does not have a soul. In their time, so much attention was focused on the soul of the home by being conscious of the materials and energy used during the building process. But the ancestors can share a wealth of information on how to call back the soul of the land.

The descendants in the future have already seen what our modern-day culture is lacking in not respecting the soul of structures, land, communities, and cities. I've found the descendants to be generous with sharing ways to heal the land and cities we live in.

If you have a shamanic journey practice, you can set your intention to journey back in time to ask helping ancestral spirits how to retrieve the soul of a piece of land, a city, or a community. You can also journey into the future and speak to the compassionate descendants. You do not need to journey to a particular ancestor or descendant. You can journey to ancestors or descendants in general, inviting in a group or an individual who is willing to share advice on designing a ceremony.

Here is the intention I use for such a journey: "Compassionate ancestors (or descendants), please come. Show me a ceremony that can be done to bring the soul of _____." Fill in the blank by identifying the structure, land, community, or city you intend to help.

Of course, you can also journey to your helping spirit to ask for a ceremony to perform.

The ceremonies that come through these journeys are quite spectacular. There is so much wisdom that the helping spirits, the ancestors, and descendants wish to share so that we can live and work in healthier environments.

If you do not journey, take a meditative walk in nature or listen to some spiritual music as you let your intuition and imagination be your guide in designing a ceremony.

ELISE GATHERS HER COMMUNITY TO PERFORM A SOUL RETRIEVAL FOR THEIR CITY

Elise designed a ceremony to return the soul of the city she lived in. She was inspired by some of the ceremonies I shared in *Welcome Home: Following Your Soul's Journey Home*. Although shy about public speaking, she found the courage to share this powerful healing work in her community.

Elise posted fliers in a variety of public places, inviting people to participate in a ceremony to call back the soul of their city. Everyone was invited to bring flowers, foods, or offerings that felt appropriate. Elise was impressed by how many people showed up for the ceremony.

Elise explained about the power of ceremony and how it could help to heal their city and community. She used an invocation with prayers that would not contradict anyone's religious beliefs.

All the offerings were placed in the middle of the circle of people that had formed. Everyone was invited to sing blessings or speak prayers into the offerings.

Individuals and families took some of the blessed offerings to leave in different parts of the city with the intention of calling the soul back of the city. They held the energy of love and deep appreciation for their city. Each offering held a message for the soul of the city to welcome it back home. Elise allotted a reasonable amount of time to spread out the offerings. She also set up a time for people to process their work and close the ceremony.

What came out of performing such a ceremony was that people who lived in the city woke up to the fact that their city had a soul that needed to be loved, honored, and respected. Elise also felt the power of working together as a community in ceremony instead of doing it alone. She and others who participated realized the issues we face on the planet today call for groups of people to work together in cooperation and collaboration to create positive change. The responsibility no longer lies in the hands of the few. The issues we are facing need our collective energy and power to improve circumstances for all in the web of life and the Earth.

A SPIRIT BOAT JOURNEY OR MEDITATION

If you work with a group, the Spirit Boat journey is a wonderful virtual ceremony you can perform. As I shared in the introduction, some of the ceremonies in this book will speak more to shamanic practitioners. Even if you are not experienced with shamanism, know that I have successfully led this practice as a guided meditation using all the elements of ceremony you've been learning.

Travel to your virtual altar, where you will be spiritually cleansed before entering in sacred space. Form a circle, appreciating the beauty of the altar—the gifts left, the candles burning, the fragrances. Invite in the compassionate spirits.

Envision a large Spirit Boat placed in the altar space by the helping spirits. This beautiful craft has seats for everyone, all facing the same direction. Note how entering this boat and facing the same way powerfully focuses your intent to work together with your group, aligning your collective energy toward a shared goal.

Once everyone is settled in the boat, journey together to the land, city, or community in need of a soul retrieval. On arrival, step out of the boat and stand on the land. Share love and appreciation for the helping ancestral spirits and the land, city, or community. Leave gifts and sing songs calling back the soul. The helping spirits might give specific directions to include in the ceremony.

Once finished, return to the boat. Continue journeying to the moon, the stars, and the sun for inspirational messages. Return with inspiration and hope to the altar room. Share how it felt to participate in the ceremony. Thank the helping spirits and return home, making sure everyone is fully back and grounded.

Working with a Spirit Boat ceremony is a powerful way to travel through the unseen realms as a group. There are many ways to improvise on this ceremony to travel as a group to perform healings on people, places, and all of life.

USING THE SPIRIT BOAT JOURNEY
IN THE PHYSICAL REALMS

The Spirit Boat journey is just as powerful when performed in a physical space. Everyone gathered in the ceremonial space sits on the floor or in chairs forming the physical outline of a boat. Each person sits touching either the shoulder or back of the person in front of them. The ceremonial leader chooses the direction for the boat, typically facing toward the place you will be journeying to.

Volunteer drummers keep up the beat, helping people stay in a nonordinary state of consciousness while they travel to do the intended healing work.

Working with a Spirit Boat in ceremony is a lovely way for a group to journey together and share their experiences as they travel to a location, to a person who is ill, to the planets, stars, and sun. Once complete, the drummers change the drumbeat to let the group know that it is time to turn the boat around and return.

BLESSINGS FOR WATER

Ceremonies can also be used to bless and heal earth, air, and water. These elements give us life. Unconscious people, businesses, and governments don't respect that if they pollute the water we drink, the earth that provides the food we eat, and the air we breathe, that all of life becomes ill. There are many bodies of water—rivers, lakes, streams, and the ocean—that are in need of deep healing because they were contaminated with toxins and waste poured into them by unconscious humans.

RETURNING THE SOUL OF THE RIO GRANDE

I was invited to present at a conference in Santa Fe. The conference was sponsored by a well-known Native American leader of the Santa Clara Pueblo. This pueblo is outside of Santa Fe and is located on the Rio Grande River. Native peoples in the Southwest believe that the Rio Grande is the main heart artery of the Earth. The health of the Rio Grande is vital to the health of the planet. Like most sacred rivers, chemicals are constantly being dumped into the Rio Grande.

The conference was small and was attended by a group of Forest Service workers who were all Hispanic. There were also members of different Native American tribes, such as the Hopi and Navajo, and a few Anglo people were also present.

I lectured on how we could perform a ceremony to call back the soul of the Rio Grande. The men present from the Forest Service snored loudly during my lecture, but once the actual ceremony began, they engaged with full passion and energy.

I brought a big bowl of water and set it on a small altar that I placed on the stage in the room. I asked everyone to gather around the bowl of water. I shared that we are a reflection of the great Creator, filled with spiritual light. I invited each person to travel inside and experience their starlight or sunlight shining through and radiating as they focused on the bowl of water and their love of the Rio Grande. Everyone was asked to perceive the water present as pristine, pure, and healthy.

I toned by chanting vowels. I find toning helps people stay focused on shining their inner light. As I toned, the Native Americans present chanted in their own languages. The Forest Service workers started praying in Spanish. Everyone was obviously moved and touched as they focused on their honor and love for the Rio Grande. Once we were all silent, I closed the ceremony.

Everyone present was asked to fill up a little bottle I provided with water from the bowl. The attendees, who had gathered from Arizona, Colorado, and New Mexico, took their bottle of water to a local spot on the Rio Grande to feed the river with the love, light, and prayers from our small circle.

I have led adaptations of the Rio Grande ceremony. Place a bowl or glass of water on your altar. Journey or meditate to experience your inner starlight or sunlight radiating through you as you perceive the water on your altar in its divine perfection and light. For beyond what is happening on a physical level, on a spiritual level, all of life on this Earth is light and perfect as it is. Tone, chant, or sit in silence, radiating your light while focusing on how much you love Water.

Afterward, bring the blessed water to a body of water where you live. If there is no local water nearby, you can imagine placing it into a body of water in the unseen realms. All water is connected and feels our love and prayers. Take a sip of this sacred water yourself. Notice how sweet and smooth it tastes. When we radiate our light, all the waters of the world light up, reflecting back our light and divinity.

12

Transforming Your Dreams
into Reality

When we make decisions to move forward with our lives, change jobs, move to a new location or home, or start a new project, we can join with the forces of the universe to ask for a positive outcome.

The Prayer Tree ceremony is a powerful way to ask for blessings as you begin a new adventure in life. You can also use the elements earth, air, water, and fire. Write a letter to God, the goddess, or the power of the universe and burn your letter or dissolve it in water while your prayers are carried to the divine forces. Groups could meet in the virtual realms at the altar, fire, or Prayer Tree and perform a blessing ceremony.

SHEREE'S CEREMONY TO ENSURE A GOOD MOVE

Sheree was leaving a job she loved and a community of close friends so that she could move closer to her aging parents to be present for their ongoing care. She found a new job near her parents and rented an apartment.

Sheree was guided to design a ceremony to draw scenes of who she was leaving, her road trip, meeting new coworkers and friends, and seeing the smiling faces of her parents.

In a ceremonial fashion, Sheree gave thanks to the spirit of the land where she lived and to the ancestors for holding her in so much love over the years. She asked her helping spirits to provide a safe trip as she drove across the country. She then journeyed to the spirit of the land where she would be living and asked the helping ancestors to welcome her to her new home, creating a graceful transition.

While in a quiet and sacred space, she created a vibrant drawing of her friends and coworkers blowing her kisses as she drove away. She drew images of landscapes she would drive through, adding clear blue skies, stunning trees and greenery, and shimmering bodies of water she would pass on her way to her new home. Next, she drew an image of herself in her new workplace, working with a smile on her face and chatting with her new coworkers. She drew her apartment with bright colors and charming decorations, including the smiling and loving faces of her parents.

Though her sketches were a bit rough, the detail or skill of her drawing did not matter. The important factor was the focus and energy she put into each image. Sheree used all her senses to experience the details of leaving her home, her road trip, and her arrival in full, vivid detail as if everything were happening now. Through her drawing, she was living her manifested dream.

Once done with her drawings, she offered each to the fire, representing that the dream was now manifested, and the work was complete.

Over the days to come, Sheree created collages with images of her new life. She began by calling in her helping spirits and letting go of the anxious thoughts that arose as she imagined starting a new life.

Sheree did manifest a good dream, and the time she got to spend with her parents at the end of their life provided some of her most precious memories.

Planting a New Garden

We all know how healthy plants grow that are fed with love. All of life is nurtured by love and care. In planting a new garden, start with your preparation work. Leave your everyday thoughts and life behind you, and move into a spiritual state of consciousness while you create sacred space. Call in the spirit of the garden. Place special rocks, statues, or crystals in your garden that hold the energy of love.

Feel the texture of the soil and smell its fragrance as you spread it and prepare it for planting. While planting your seeds or new plants, sing to them. All of nature sings and loves to be sung to. If you fully open your invisible senses, you can see your plants glow after singing to them and hear them singing back to you.

When you water, perceive the water as filled with light and love that will nurture growth.

In all spiritual cultures, "weed" is not considered a proper term to use, for these plants embrace high vibrational medicine. But if there is a plant you wish to remove from your garden, do it with love and care. Thank it for growing in your garden, even though you might struggle physically to pull it out to be composted.

Imagine the foods you cook and create from what grows in your garden. You want to ingest food that has grown filled with love. There is an entire process that occurs, from planting in healthy soil, nurturing your garden over time, and picking your plants with intention.

Incorporating the elements of ceremony allows you to honor your garden as a sacred space.

In most shamanic cultures, there is a belief in what I call the Hidden Folk. They can be talked about as devas, fairies, elves, angels, forest guardians, sprites, and other terms. These beings can be quite tall or so small that they're barely visible.

These nature beings live in cities as well as in the country. They are caretakers of the Earth and are quite protective of the environments we live in. They have little trust for humans, as they have watched humans destroy their environments and nature.

But they will still respond if you call them with invocations, songs, and offerings. Once they are called in, they will join you in your ceremonial work of tending your garden. There are many famous stories about healthy and exquisite gardens that grow with the help of the Hidden Folk.

I have also collected a wealth of stories from students who have journeyed to the Hidden Folk. Once home from a workshop, they actively engage with the Hidden Folk in growing and tending their gardens. I receive stellar reports on the size and vitality of the fruits, vegetables, and flowers that are grown in partnership with the Hidden Folk. But you will need to earn their trust by showing that you are committed to being a caretaker of the Earth.

You might join with others where you live to plant a community garden. Everyone who engages can benefit from practicing love, respect, and honor for the spirit of the garden. Imagine the quality of food the children and families will eat. What we ingest affects both our emotional and physical health, since we also ingest the energy we shared while tending our plants.

You can learn to see all land as a garden. After a catastrophic event, to call back the soul of land or to simply honor the land, you can scatter seeds imbued with the love and light in your breath. In this way, you cultivate our home, the Earth.

Damini, a brilliant shamanic teacher, created a remarkable ceremony of placing prayers for the Earth in clay pods and planting them in different locations. She calls her clay containers PrayerPods, and they dissolve over time into the earth. To learn more about this project, you can visit the website listed in the resource section at the end of this book. This ceremony has caught on with some of my students, who are planting clay prayer pods all over the world. All materials used are environmentally safe.

REQUESTING PROTECTION AND SUPPORT

There are times when we feel vulnerable and want spiritual support. By performing solo or group ceremonies, we can request the protection of the compassionate spirits and the divine.

You can use ribbons or yarn tied on a Prayer Tree to ask for protection and support. You can also adapt such a ceremony and use prayer bowls in which you, your loved ones, coworkers, or community members can place prayers for protection, blessing, support, and healing. Blowing bubbles or prayers into the wind while requesting protection is a wonderful way to work because the wind is such a powerful ally.

FRANK PREPARES FOR HEART SURGERY

Frank was preparing for heart surgery. His health was compromised, and his family and friends were worried about him. His family lived in multiple cities, and it was not possible for them to physically gather for a ceremony.

Frank's daughter Amy led a ceremony on his behalf. She sent an invitation for his family to tune in via videoconferencing. Amy asked everyone assembled to imagine themselves walking to the altar room where they were spiritually cleansed and invited to gather in a circle.

Amy asked Frank's family and friends to state a blessing or prayer for him as well as to imagine the surgeon and all the staff in their divine light and strength. They all imagined Frank coming through the surgery with grace and ease.

In the guided meditation, Amy instructed everyone to put their prayers for Frank into bowls on the altar. Amy also called in Frank's helping spirits to care for him during the surgery.

Frank was not well enough to attend, but he was touched to hear the stories from his family about the work performed on his behalf. He went into the surgery feeling completely supported, and this helped alleviate his fears and instill hope. By going into surgery with such a positive attitude, he found he brightened up his medical team. The surgery went very well, and he even had an unexpectedly rapid recovery afterward.

A PROTECTION CEREMONY FOR DERRICK AS HE LEAVES FOR WAR

Dakota's brother Derrick was about to go into the army. Nobody knew where he would be deployed. Derrick's friends and family were anxious about how he'd cope in the military.

Dakota created a ceremony, bringing in brightly colored candles. She created a sacred space in the family home, and everyone who attended performed their preparation in ways that felt right to them. After their preparation work, some of their anxiety melted away, and a sense of trust permeated the energy in the room. They now felt that Derrick would be in the hands of loving spirits and the divine.

Each person lit a candle while stating decrees and prayers, such as, "Derrick is held in the loving arms of the universe" and "Thank you for bringing Derrick back home safely."

Derrick absorbed the words of blessings, prayers, and decrees. He felt supported by his loved ones and his community. This made a huge difference, as he knew how much he was loved and knew there would be people praying for him throughout his service.

The light of the candles represented how Derrick's path would be lit and the love of his community. Everyone made a commitment to keep candles burning until Derrick no longer needed support and could be welcomed home by his friends and family.

This is a lovely ceremony to do for anyone who is about to have surgery, leaving for war, or facing a life transition.

ANGELA PROTECTS HERSELF FROM TOXIC ENERGIES

Angela was greatly impacted by the toxic energy of some of her coworkers. Angela had learned to call in her helping spirits before work each day and to surround herself in protective blue light. Even so, she dreaded sitting in the collective field of toxic energy during many office meetings.

When she knew there was a meeting on her agenda, Angela performed a ceremony at her home altar. She lit a candle, whistled, and rattled to greet and honor her helping spirits. She asked for special protection during any upcoming meeting that she felt would be unpleasant.

She normally felt drained and ill after she left her meetings. Yet she found that when she performed a ceremony to ask for protection beforehand, she felt held in a protective bubble, and the negative energies had no impact on her. She even began to hear telepathic messages from her helping spirits to speak certain words or present ideas during the meeting to transform the negative energy. She learned how to perform a simplified version of her ceremony spontaneously at the office whenever she needed protection.

This same type of ceremony is useful when you feel a need for protection while driving or flying, and while doing other activities where you are in a collective energetic space or field that feels toxic. If you don't have time for preparation, you can easily perform a spontaneous ceremony by simply asking for help and offering your prayers in a sacred way.

ALIGNING OURSELVES WITH THE CYCLES OF NATURE

We are nature. We often perceive ourselves as separate, but we are part of the web of life that connects us all. And all of life is impacted by the changing cycles and phases in nature. Nature is our best teacher about birth and rebirth, dismemberment, dissolution, rememberment, and illumination. For all of life dies, leading to the rebirth of new life. A grove of trees might die, but new trees, plants, and grasses grow in its place.

It saddens us to watch death, and we certainly grieve over losing loved ones, friends, and beings in nature that we love. But birth and death are part of life. Creating sacred ceremonies during seasonal and lunar changes helps us navigate the changes within and without.

It is important to celebrate the sunrise, sunset, new and full moon, and seasonal changes as connected rather than separate. When we observe the changes in the quality of light between the sunrise and sunset, changing phases of the moon, and seasons, we reconnect to a sense of organic flow and how all life experiences are woven together.

Exercise to Connect with Nature's Flow

Stand in nature. Close your eyes and notice in your body how everything in nature is moving and flowing. When I was growing up, I used to watch cartoons showing the sun, trees, and plants singing and dancing gracefully. This is actually what occurs in nature. Every season, lunar cycle, and transition is part of a great flow. Feel this flow of nature as you rock back and forth and from side to side.

Once you enter this state, you can feel the need to enter the flow of life instead of trying to control it. Nature's flow cannot be controlled. Once you learn how to surrender and move with the flow, health returns on all levels as you walk with the flow of life instead of against it.

In shamanic cultures, songs would be sung daily to greet and give gratitude to the rising sun and honor the setting sun. As you honor the changing light, you honor your own internal changes.

No matter where you live, you experience the four phases of the changing seasons. You can observe changes in the landscape, migration patterns of birds, and the appearance of certain animals. You witness the death of older life-forms in autumn and winter, giving rise to new plants, trees, flowers, and baby nature beings in the spring and summer.

Become attuned to times of the year when nature is more expansive and expressive, and to times when growth around us slows down, lets go of the old, and turns within for regeneration. Discover how the light changes at different times of the year. Notice how the texture and the quality of the air feels different as the seasons flow into each other. This helps you reflect on your personal cycles, so you can align with the seasonal changes within and without.

The moon cycles from newness to fullness. Become aware of how this cycle deeply impacts you physically and emotionally. Our bodies are mostly water. Just as the lunar phases change the tides, you can feel these changes happening inside of you.

The new moon is seen as a time of new beginnings. It is a time to experience rebirth and begin working on new endeavors, such as welcoming in a new relationship, starting a new project or job, or moving into a new home. Imagine yourself looking up at the night sky and seeing the sliver of the new moon. You can feel the strength of rebirth.

As the moon waxes, nurture what you began during the new moon.

For many, the full moon is a powerful time to perform ceremonies and healing work. This is a time when the energy of the moon is strongest. During the full moon, people's moods change; hospitals and police stations get busier. People do not know what to do with their energy. A wonderful way to channel this energy is to perform a ceremony on the full moon, to honor the moon and to perform healing and blessing work. The abundance of power makes the full moon a potent time to gather groups through virtual ceremonies and work together in service to the Earth.

Once we move into the phase of the waning moon, we can take a breath and relax before a new cycle begins.

When you tune in to the phases of the moon, you may notice that your creativity and activities are supported during certain phases. We are all unique beings, and your cycles might be different from anyone else's. Be open to discovery as you explore how the phases of the moon support your needs.

Most of us live fast-paced lives, and we are not aware of how our physical energy and our mood changes with the seasons and lunar cycles. When we slow down and perform ceremonies to honor the flow of life within and without, we learn how to follow the cycles of nature. When we reconnect to the lunar cycles and changes in the seasons, we feel more embodied and attuned with our connection to the Earth.

There are many ceremonies you can perform to honor the changes in nature and your inner cycles. They can be as simple as taking a ceremonial walk. Find a tree, body of water, or sacred place where you would like to leave some offerings while giving thanks to earth, air, water, sun, and moon for providing all you need to thrive physically, emotionally, and spiritually.

Spirit Boat Ceremony to Honor Nature's Cycles

You can perform the Spirit Boat journey for yourself or with a group to travel into the unseen realms and learn from a celestial body like the moon or sun. Refer to "A Spirit Boat Journey or Meditation" in chapter 11 to make your preparations.

As a group of travelers wishing to honor the moon or sun, travel to these great sources and speak to them. Share messages that are not only personal for the journeyer, but for the entire group about how to align with the changing phases of the cycles of nature. Sing songs of appreciation along the way to honor the moon and sun. Singing is an inherent part of shamanic practice and ceremony. Allow your own songs and chants to flow through you, or sing songs you have learned from others as you honor all of nature.

You can also do this ceremony in a virtual format to bring friends and peers together during the changing phases. This creates a way to share spiritual knowledge while giving you a container to perform spiritual work and ceremonies while living in different locations.

Spending Time in Nature

Bringing a ceremonial frame of mind to your time in nature infuses the simplest acts with sacredness. As the seasons change and the moon progresses through her phases, take time to stand outside. Let the sun bathe you during the day and take a moon bath at night. Feel the radiance of these life-giving forces bathing and healing you. This is such a powerful and simple ceremony you can perform alone or with a group.

CINDY HONORS THE CHANGE IN SEASONS

Cindy felt her body was out of balance, and she could not find a natural rhythm in her life. She felt sure this imbalance was the source of many of her health challenges, so she made a commitment to restore her inner harmony by honoring the change in seasons.

On the equinoxes and solstices, Cindy spent time in nature. When she could manage it, she would spend an entire day enjoying nature. When her work schedule only allowed her an hour or two, she still took the time to set aside her everyday worries and spend sacred time in her favorite park.

Cindy wrote poems about the exquisite healing quality of nature. Before leaving her house, she always put on her special ceremonial scarf and brought the small sacred rattle she'd made. These sacred objects were unobtrusive and could be taken anywhere. Cindy would sit with her favorite tree and read her poem in a soft voice filled with loving words and acceptance of the new qualities the equinox or solstice would bring into her life. She left offerings at the tree while giving thanks to the compassionate ancestors of the land; earth, air, water, and fire; the sun, the moon, her helping spirits, and the Earth itself for guiding her during the changing times so that she could harmonize with the changes within.

Cindy walked ceremoniously while gazing at the changing leaves of the trees and plants. She would notice how the texture, feel, and smell in the air seemed different with each season. She listened to the new birdsong that emerged at different times of the year. She loved to watch the activity of the small animals in the park, especially in fall as they busily prepared for winter. She enjoyed walking in nature in the spring when she might catch glimpses of newborn squirrels and chipmunks. When alone, she danced to feel the inherent flow of nature and the heartbeat of the Earth. She was inspired by the spiritual messages the wind carried to her.

Cindy sang to the moon as it changed phases, waiting for the moon to sing back to her. She received messages of how to change her level of activity, placing her in sync with the moon's changing rhythms. She received a wealth of omens.

Through her ongoing ceremonial work, Cindy regained her health. She felt in a harmonious flow instead of always feeling out of step.

INTEGRATING CEREMONY INTO YOUR LIFE

Many shamanic and spiritual practitioners choose to perform their releasing and blessing ceremonies during the new moon and full moon, and on the equinoxes and solstices. Spiritual energies are abundant to support ceremonies as we release challenges, ask for blessings in starting a new project, or face a life transition. As we ask for assistance, we also celebrate the phase of the moon, equinox, or solstice through our invocations, songs, and dances.

Bring your ceremonial work during changing seasons to your favorite place and sing, write letters to the Earth, and receive messages of deep wisdom. For example, if you live near an ocean, try performing a ceremony on the shore. The ocean is a powerful source of love and wisdom. There is so much to learn by watching the ocean, listening to the sound of the waves, smelling the salt in the air, and feeling the humidity. Standing with bare feet on the sand while performing a ceremony in which people sing to the ocean, talk to it, and listen for messages is heartwarming and inspiring.

We experience earth, air, water, and fire outside of our body, but our organs are also earth, air, water, and fire. When honoring the changes in nature through our ceremonial work, we honor the changes within each of us. We return to honoring nature in ways that shamans have worked with for thousands of years to establish harmony between nature and the community.

DAILY CEREMONIES

Just as you honor the land and all of life during seasonal changes and lunar phases, realize that every day is a natural cycle. Each day, you can integrate simple ceremonies to express gratitude and respect for the land where you live; the nature beings; the elements of earth, air, water, and fire; and your life.

Life is a ceremony. I put my attention into my daily activities and how I work with my consciousness throughout the day to bring the sacred into everything that I do.

Upon awakening, I give gratitude—even if I'm not feeling well or not looking forward to what's on my schedule. I start with giving gratitude for my life and to earth, air, water, and sun, which provide life. I give thanks for what I do have in my life instead of focusing on what is not working. I perform a ceremonial prayer: I sit at my altar, light a candle, set my intention for the day, and ask that any challenging event goes well.

Create simple ceremonies by leaving offerings at a small outside altar. Walk the land and sing, drum, or rattle while expressing your gratitude. Or find a spot to sit and do the same.

I created a Prayer Tree to leave prayers for those in need and for the Earth. I also like to leave offerings at a tree that I call my "ritual tree," where I can express gratitude to the ancestors of the land; the Spirit of Santa Fe; earth, air, water, and fire (as the sun); the Hidden Folk; the spirit of the forest; my helping spirits; and my own ancestors. I might not always do this outside ritual daily, but I always wake up and express gratitude for my life and all in the web of life.

I cook in a ceremonial fashion. As I chop vegetables and prepare food, I focus on who I am cooking for and the power of love I want to infuse into the food. Cooking is a ceremony. It is not a time for me to think about who or what is making me angry or about what is not working in my life and in the world. Cooking is a healing ceremony because as we eat food, we absorb the love of life. As I wash dishes, I give thanks to water and all the nourishment that water brings to me and all of life.

Singing while you cook brings in sacred ceremony to preparing your food. Blessing your food as you eat is a way to absorb the goodness that the Earth and the elements provide.

Reflect on ways that you can bring the elements of ceremony into your daily activities. You will find your life becoming enriched as you bring the sacred into all parts of your day.

Blessing ceremonies can be adapted and improvised to honor birthdays, anniversaries, and holidays. This is a beautiful way to honor transitions and holy times, and to turn them into sacred events.

BLESSING CEREMONY FOR THE
WEB OF LIGHT AND THE EARTH

Most readers of this book likely have a concern for the environmental, political, and terrorist challenges we face during these turbulent times. We want to find ways in which we can be in service to all of life and the Earth.

We want to protect the exquisite life-forms in the web of life—the animals and birds, sea creatures, invertebrates, reptiles, insects, trees, plants, moss, plankton, rocks, crystals, microorganisms, and the elements.

Since 2000, I have been teaching a practice and a ceremony called transfiguration. The understanding behind this ceremony is that our authentic Self is spiritual light. We are beings of divine light, clothed by our body and mind.

When we travel within to our inner landscape and experience our inner starlight, sunlight, or flame, we can allow that light to flow into our cells, creating emotional and physical healing.

As we let that divine light radiate through us like a star in the night sky or like the shining sun, we stimulate the light in our loved ones, others around us, all in the web of the life, and the Earth itself.

This process came to me in a dream in which the Egyptian god Anubis shared with me that the missing element of my spiritual work to reverse environmental pollution is transfiguration. After processing this message, I started to teach transfiguration to groups around the world. I've written about this in some of my books, including *Medicine for the Earth* and *Walking in Light*.

At my workshops, we've scientifically measured the effects of transfiguration work. We placed toxic substances on our altar and placed people who were ill in the middle of our circle. We used a GDV (gas discharge visualization) camera, which captures images and measures changes in the field of energy. We also tracked pH changes in ammonium hydroxide, a solution of ammonia dissolved in water.

It was clear that the work of transfiguration produced powerful and positive results in both working with environmental toxins and with people who were facing physical challenges.

The process of transfiguration is a feminine process of creating positive changes by "being" instead of "doing." It's a common spiritual teaching that to experience peace in the world, you must be peaceful within. Our outer world reflects our inner state of consciousness.

With the process of transfiguration, you do not try to heal the environment, a community, loved ones, clients, nature beings, the Earth, and so on. Rather, you experience your own spiritual and divine light and let that radiate like a star or the sun. The stars and sun do not labor to generate light or choose where that light goes. They simply radiate and brighten up all of life.

Our perception creates our reality. We can perceive others and the planet as sick and toxic, or we can perceive all of life in its strength and as spiritual light. Focusing on the spiritual light and strength in others empowers their own process of healing. When we radiate our light and perceive all of life and the Earth as light, healing happens. It is quite an extraordinary process.

In many parts of the world, shamans work with radiating light as their way of healing. I personally have found that this way of working helps us evolve our consciousness and create a higher vibration and frequency in ourselves and in our outer world.

You can develop a transfiguration practice for yourself. This is not a shamanic journey, so you don't need to have any experience with shamanism. Start with your ceremonial preparation work and create sacred space. Listen to some spiritual or uplifting music.

When you are ready, imagine yourself traveling within into your inner landscape and experience yourself as a star, the sun, or a flame. Imagine your body and mind dissolving, so you are in unity and one with all of life and with the divine forces of the universe.

Let that light flow through you and be absorbed by all your cells, like a flower absorbs the light of the sun to be healthy, vital, and vibrant. If you do this on a regular basis for even fifteen to twenty minutes at a time, you will notice a shift in your health on all levels.

You can add a step and imagine that light radiating within and throughout the Earth. This shifts the perception of toxicity to one of health, love, and light. Radiate your light, holding the focus on where you feel concern.

Do not send this light—just let it radiate. You are not actively trying to heal another or a place, so you do not need permission from others to see them in their light. You simply perceive all in their divine light instead of perceiving suffering and toxicity. This shift in perception makes a difference.

Some people, including myself, can have a different experience of transfiguring. We may experience ourselves as the darkness of the void instead of the light of a star or the sun. This is just as powerful in its own way. In shamanism and many spiritual traditions, the void is recognized as the place before creation. It is seen as empty, yet full. It is rich and fertile. All that is created in the invisible realms through our thoughts, words, and daydreams originates in the void. It is a deep and potent place to work with if your transfiguration practice leads you there.

The transfiguration ceremony is so powerful and easy to perform that many of my students and readers of my monthly column and my books have brought this work into their communities and groups. Some bring the practice into their family lives. Children love to transfigure. Give them the instruction to dance like a star, and they move right into radiating their light. They get it!

There are numerous groups who meet in their local communities to perform monthly transfiguration ceremonies. Some groups have fifty to sixty people who show up each month. Some groups regularly meet in a virtual space to practice transfiguration for places on the Earth in need. Names of places and people can be placed in bowls on the altar in ordinary reality or in the virtual realms. During the transfiguration work, each person radiates light to a person or place in need. You can place a globe or crystal sculpture of the Earth in the virtual altar room as a focus.

Below is a ceremony I have led in workshops and conferences. I have led this ceremony at many events, some with more than eight hundred people with diverse backgrounds and beliefs in attendance. I use the same ceremony in smaller groups. Perform this transfiguration ceremony indoors or outside.

Please feel free to use this ceremony among your friends, loved ones, and in your local community. You can use it as it is or make changes as you are guided to keep the ceremony relevant to the group you are working with.

I added toning to the ceremony, as I find it helps most people to stay focused on radiating their light. Otherwise, when people move into the ecstatic state of the shaman, their experience of being divine light and in unity with the power of the universe can get disrupted by the rational mind. Toning works well to keep hearts open and minds focused on the ceremony.

TRANSFIGURATION CEREMONY

We are spirit. If we allow our spiritual light to shine through, we become a healing presence. Take a few deep breaths. We do this for every living being and the Earth itself.

I whistle and rattle to begin before drumming.

Take a few deep breaths and let your thoughts drift away. As you breathe, place your hands on your heart. Feel and get in touch with your heartbeat. With our heartbeat, let's connect with the heartbeat of everyone present in the room who has gathered together on behalf of all of life and the Earth.

Let's connect our heartbeat to the heartbeat of the spirit of the land where we are gathered and the helping ancestors who have loved this land so much and who join in our work. Connect with the heartbeat of Mother Earth.

You are body, mind, and spirit. When you let go of the body and your daily thoughts, your mind, who you are beyond your skin, is spiritual light. Before you were born, you were just a tiny being of spiritual light looking down on this great Earth, and you were excited about this incredible adventure of being born into a body that can manifest spirit into form, just like the Creator and the creative forces of the universe.

I invite you to travel inside to your Inner World. Imagine traveling within and experience your light. Our light is like the beauty of the night sky. Our light is like starlight. Stars don't try to shine. They radiate effortlessly. They don't say, "I think I am only going to shine on this one place on the Earth." They don't send their light—they shine.

Our light is like the sun. Our spirit is like the sun that shines above us, feeding all of life with the energy to thrive, unconditionally, never asking for anything in return. Experience your own inner sunlight. Our light is like a flame.

Travel within your Inner World and experience yourself merging with a star or the sun. Or experiencing a flame and absorb the light into your cells like a flower that absorbs sunlight or like a plant or tree that soaks in the rain. Let that light flow through you.

Without effort, let that light radiate while connecting our lights together. Experience that light radiating within and throughout this entire Earth, touching all of life.

I invite you to stand with your hands and palms facing our Earth. I use a photo of the Earth for the group to focus on.

As you stand, allow that light to effortlessly radiate through you while we tone together the sound of creation.

I give examples of "om" or just singing a vowel, letting it flow into other vowels: "o ah eee ooh."

When it is time to end, I fade out the drumming. I use chimes, a Tibetan bowl, or bells to signal it is time to stop toning.

Take a few deep breaths. While it is important to feel grounded, do not disconnect from your light, because you *are* light. As you still feel that light radiating through you, experience your body and the preciousness of being in a body. It is a gift to have a body and to live on this Earth.

Imagine deep roots going down into the earth, grounding you. Feel your heartbeat still connected to the heartbeat of all life. We do this work for ourselves, and we do it on behalf of the web of life and the Earth itself. We can all be a presence of healing and create positive change for all of life and the planet.

End the ceremony, and thank everyone for coming.

In the practice of shamanism, life is seen as a ceremony. When we bring the sacred into all our activities—into how we think about ourselves, others, and the world—and create sacred space, we improve the quality of our own lives and bless all of life at the same time. Performing ceremonies creates beautiful healing and changes, and brings to us the goodness of life. You will feel empowered in your work to help yourself, others, and the Earth. Performing ceremonies is good medicine!

As humans are evolving so quickly, I am excited for the future generations who will carry on ceremonial work to help their community and all of life thrive.

13

Joining Together to Bless
Our Global Community

Thousands of people will join you in reading *The Book of Ceremony*. By performing the ceremonies I have described, or by improvising your own, you will join a beautiful collective field of energy of like-minded people, all working to be in service to all of life and the Earth.

I invite you, in your own time, to perform the following blessing ceremony to hold our collective in support, love, and light. In the practice of shamanism, we work outside of time. It does not matter when you perform this ceremony, as the power of the collective energies builds as each person joins in.

Listen to a favorite drumming or shamanic music track that can support you. Drum, rattle, sing, and dance. After you have read the instructions of the ceremony a few times, continue to work in your own way.

OUR COLLECTIVE BLESSING CEREMONY

Place your hands on your heart. Think about something in life that you are in awe and wonder of. We all have something that is precious to us. Maybe it is your favorite flower or another nature being. What is your favorite fragrance or your favorite taste? What are your favorite sounds? Place what is special to you in your heart.

As you breathe, step away from your ordinary thoughts and concerns. It is a privilege to join together as a dedicated collective in service to life and the Earth. Imagine stepping into a loving circle. Breathe deeply and connect to your heartbeat.

Connect to the heartbeat of the Earth. We are always connected to the Earth's heartbeat. Connect to the spirit of the land where you live. The more you connect with the land where you live, the more gracefully your life will flow. As you connect with the helping ancestral spirits of the land you live on, your ceremonial work will be more fluid and successful.

Feel the power, love, and the spiritual light of our virtual circle. We can't see each other, but we can feel the presence of each other with our nonordinary senses. Feel the power, the love, and the spiritual light flowing through you. Welcome each other from the heart. No matter how you are feeling right now, no matter what is going on in your life, you are welcome in our circle.

We welcome and greet our helping compassionate spirits, divine forces, and the spirit of earth, air, water, and fire, as the sun. We greet the spirit that lives in all things, as well as the moon and the stars. We know the creative power of the words we use.

In shamanism, it is well understood that thoughts are things. Our thoughts feed into the dreams that manifest in our physical world.

Close your eyes and focus on your heart.

Imagine yourself standing up from the place where you are journeying or meditating. Step out of your front door. As you do this, imagine yourself lifting a veil between the ordinary world to the power of the unseen realms. As you lift the veil between the worlds, you step out onto a beautiful path in nature.

Walk the path surrounded by trees or through your favorite landscape. Feel the earth beneath you. Reach down and touch the soil, the rock, or the sand, and feel its texture. Gaze upon the surrounding beauty. Observe the greenery, the rocks, the animals, the insects, the flowers, and other nature beings. Feel the wind cleansing you and embracing you in love.

What a gift to live on this amazing planet. What a gift to be in community, working through our personal and planetary challenges together. No matter how dark we feel as we walk the path, there is always light ahead. In nature, there is always the darkness and the light. There is always death and then rebirth. There is the dissolution and then the illumination.

Continue walking. Take a deep breath and smell the fragrances. Listen to the sounds of nature and taste the air. Notice how you are feeling right now as you do this.

Arrive at a meadow where you are greeted by guardian spirits waiting for you. As you are greeted, one of the guardian spirits will spiritually cleanse you. The guardian spirit might use incense to cleanse you or a feather to wipe away anything that needs to be cleared. Before you move into sacred and holy space, you have to let go of your burdens for any ceremony to be successful.

As you are cleansed, notice that there is a powerful fire burning in the middle of this meadow. Enter a circle forming around the fire. Imagine yourself drumming, singing, dancing, or remaining silent.

Smell the fire. Listen to the crackling sounds of the wood burning. As we stand together in the circle, let's take a moment to look around and gaze into each other's eyes, see the light, and feel the love of every person in our circle. We have gathered outside of time to bless each other, to stand strong together in unity and in love for ourselves, for all of life, and for the Earth.

Notice bowls filled with sticks that have yarn wrapped around them. Walk up to one of the bowls and pick up a stick that has yarn of your favorite color. Notice the color you have picked, what it means to you, and how it makes you feel on a cellular level. Travel within and imagine a word whose vibration holds beauty, power, and love. The vibration will travel up into the universe and will manifest back on the Earth.

Blow the power of this word into your prayer stick. As you do that, walk up to the fire and put your prayer stick in the flames with the intention of blessing yourself, our community who has gathered together in their own time, all of life, and the Earth.

As you place your prayer stick into the fire, the fire will share this blessing with the creative forces of the universe. The universe will join you in partnership in this blessing ceremony. After placing your prayer stick into the fire, notice that there are sacred herbs to feed the fire with. Place some herbs into the fire in gratitude and return to the circle. Gaze into the eyes of each person, seeing their light shining through. Experience the vibration of unity.

Let the love and light you are feeling flow. As you look around the circle, state out loud the word you chose to bless our circle. I will join you as you do this, as I share the words "exquisite," "magic," and "luminescence." Let's hold hands and continue to feel the power of love and light flowing through our entire circle.

As humans, we are the bridge between Earth and Sky. We bridge the power of the universe through our hearts. Feel the love flowing. Let us be that bridge of love as we stand strong together in service to the planet. Once again, look at the beauty of the fire and of nature.

It is now time for us to take our leave. Let's give thanks to our circle and drop hands.

Walk back down the beautiful path in nature into the room that you are journeying or meditating in. Thank the helping spirits and divine forces called in, who have supported your work and who have held you in unconditional love. Step through the veil of the unseen realms into your ordinary space.

Notice how you are feeling. Ground yourself by feeling deep roots connecting you with the earth.

Breathe deeply and open your eyes. Our work is done for now.

When you've completed this ceremony, you might choose to put your word of blessing on your altar, continuing to bless our circle and all of life, holding us all in love. Remember, we are in one global Spirit Boat, supporting each other as we ride together through the good weather and the storms that life brings.

ACKNOWLEDGMENTS

This book would not have been possible without all my peers, friends, students, and readers of my monthly columns and books joining me in performing ceremonies for personal and global healing. I learned so much from performing ceremonies alone and with groups. I also have been inspired by how many of my students have taken up sharing ceremonies with their friends, loved ones, coworkers, and communities.

I have felt honored and inspired by hearing from my students about their improvisations and adaptations of ceremonies I teach. It is quite extraordinary to learn about the innovative and powerful ceremonies they are performing in their circles and communities.

So, I thank my global community for joining me in this transformative and ecstatic work.

I also want to thank my agent, Barbara Moulton, who has been such a support to me personally and professionally.

I give my deepest gratitude to Tami Simon and Jaime Schwalb at Sounds True for inviting me to write *The Book of Ceremony*. Performing ceremonies is a true passion of mine, and it has been a delight to write this book.

To add to the gift of writing *The Book of Ceremony*, I had the joy to work with both Grayson Towler and Haven Iverson as my editors. I believe Grayson is a brilliant shamanic practitioner, and I loved the issues he brought up as a shamanic teacher himself. He gave me a lot to think about and reflect on as we explored how to make this book accessible to people traveling diverse spiritual paths. And I give thanks to all the staff at Sounds True who helped with the editing and final phases of the book.

I feel honored to have Mitchell Clute at Sounds True, who is an amazing writer and shamanic teacher, as an ally. His expansive worldview of life and shamanism brings me home when I lose my orientation.

I also give gratitude to Sylvia Edwards for her friendship and immense support in all levels of my life. Her presence in my life is an invaluable gift I cannot put words to.

And to my husband, Woods Shoemaker, thank you for who you are, your brilliant light, and unconditional love. I love the ceremony of life we have created together.

RESOURCES

The following resources for learning the practice of shamanic journeying can be found on sandraingerman.com.

BOOKS

- *Shamanic Journeying: A Beginner's Guide*

- *Awakening to the Spirit World: The Shamanic Path of Direct Revelation* (coauthored with Hank Wesselman)

- *Walking in Light: The Everyday Empowerment of a Shamanic Life*

AUDIO PROGRAMS

- *The Beginner's Guide to Shamanic Journeying*

- *Shamanic Meditations: Guided Journeys for Insight, Vision, and Healing*

- *Shamanic Visioning: Connecting with Spirit to Transform Your Inner and Outer Worlds*

Music

- *Soul Journeys: Music for Shamanic Practice*

- *Shamanic Visioning Music: Taiko Drum Journeys*

- *The Spirit of Healing: Shamanic Journey Music*
  (coauthored with Byron Metcalf)

Journal Article

- You can order the published pilot research I conducted with the University of Michigan's Integrative Medicine program to show how my "Medicine for the Earth" practices can be helpful for those who have suffered a heart attack.

- Sara L. Warber et al., "Healing the Heart: A Randomized Pilot Study of a Spiritual Retreat for Depression in Acute Coronary Syndrome Patients," *Explore* 7, no. 4 (2011): 222–33, doi: 10.1016/j.explore.2011.04.002.

Online Classes (under "Trainings")

- *Experiencing the Shamanic Journey: A Direct Path of Revelation* (produced by Sounds True). A weekend workshop I taught on shamanic journeying in Boulder, Colorado. Also available at soundstrue.com/store/health-healing/experiencing-the-shamanic-journey-2423.html.

- *Shamanic Journeying for Guidance and Healing: Opening to Love, Beauty, and Wisdom Through Sacred Ceremony and Community* parts 1 and 2 (produced by the Shift Network).

A seven- and twelve-week teleconferencing course you can take at any time. Also available at shamanicjourneyingcourse.com.

More Resources for Your Ceremony Work

- **Shamanic Teachers and Workshops**   I have been training teachers internationally since 2003. On shamanicteachers.com, I list brilliant teachers and practitioners from around the world. You can also find out more about workshops on shamanic journeying, personal and planetary healing, and guidance for living a shamanic life. You can contact a local shamanic teacher or practitioner on this list to help you design or perform a ceremony in your community, for healing, or to take a workshop.

- **The Transmutation App (available for Android and iOS)** I created this app to help you to shift negative thoughts to those that lead to your desired outcome. You can set an alert that asks you to reflect on what you are thinking about throughout the day and that inspires you to shift your thoughts by viewing words, phrases, blessings, and photos provided in the included library. This is a great app to keep you focused on integrating sacred ceremony into your daily life. You can download the Transmutation app from iTunes, Amazon, or Google Play.

- **Dissolving Paper**   You can purchase dissolving paper on sciencebobstore.com. This paper is made of cellulose and dissolves in water, steam, and most aqueous solutions. It is biodegradable, nontoxic, and safe for the environment.

- **Damini Celebre's PrayerPods**   You can learn about this project by visiting daminicelebre.com/prayer-pods.

About the Author

Sandra Ingerman, MA, is an award-winning author of twelve books, including *Soul Retrieval: Mending the Fragmented Self*; *Medicine for the Earth: How to Transform Personal and Environmental Toxins*; and *Walking in Light: The Everyday Empowerment of a Shamanic Life*. She is the presenter of eight audio programs produced by Sounds True, and she is the creator of the Transmutation app.

Sandra is a world-renowned teacher of shamanism and has been teaching for more than thirty-five years. She has taught workshops internationally on shamanic journeying, healing, and reversing environmental pollution using spiritual methods. Sandra is recognized for bridging ancient cross-cultural healing methods to our modern culture, addressing the needs of our times.

Sandra is devoted to teaching people how to work together as a global community to bring about positive change for the planet. She is passionate about helping people reconnect with nature.

Sandra is a licensed marriage and family therapist and professional mental health counselor. She is also a board-certified expert on traumatic stress. She was awarded the 2007 Peace Award from the Global Foundation for Integrative Medicines. Sandra was chosen as one of the Top Ten Spiritual Heroes of 2013 by *Spirituality & Health* magazine.

sandraingerman.com

shamanicteachers.com

ABOUT SOUNDS TRUE

Sounds True is a multimedia publisher whose mission is to inspire and support personal transformation and spiritual awakening. Founded in 1985 and located in Boulder, Colorado, we work with many of the leading spiritual teachers, thinkers, healers, and visionary artists of our time. We strive with every title to preserve the essential "living wisdom" of the author or artist. It is our goal to create products that not only provide information to a reader or listener, but that also embody the quality of a wisdom transmission.

For those seeking genuine transformation, Sounds True is your trusted partner. At SoundsTrue.com you will find a wealth of free resources to support your journey, including exclusive weekly audio interviews, free downloads, interactive learning tools, and other special savings on all our titles.

To learn more, please visit SoundsTrue.com/freegifts or call us toll-free at 800.333.9185.

SOUNDS TRUE
many voices, one journey